New Perspectives on
Creating Web Pages with

Netscape Navigator™ Gold Software

B R I E F

Patrick M. Carey
Carey Associates, Inc.

COURSE
TECHNOLOGY

ONE MAIN STREET, CAMBRIDGE, MA 02142

an International Thomson Publishing company I(T)P®

Cambridge • Albany • Bonn • Boston • Cincinnati • London • Madrid • Melbourne • Mexico City
New York • Paris • San Francisco • Singapore • Tokyo • Toronto • Washington

New Perspectives on Creating Web Pages with Netscape Navigator Gold Software is published by Course Technology.

Associate Publisher	Mac Mendelsohn
Series Consulting Editor	Susan Solomon
Product Manager	Joan Carey
Production Editor	Christine Spillett
Text and Cover Designer	Ella Hannah
Cover Illustrator	Doug Goodman

© 1997 by Course Technology – I(T)P®

For more information contact:

Course Technology
One Main Street
Cambridge, MA 02142

International Thomson Publishing Europe
Berkshire House 168-173
High Holborn
London WCIV 7AA
England

Thomas Nelson Australia
102 Dodds Street
South Melbourne, 3205
Victoria, Australia

Nelson Canada
1120 Birchmount Road
Scarborough, Ontario
Canada M1K 5G4

International Thomson Editores
Campos Eliseos 385, Piso 7
Col. Polanco
11560 Mexico D.F. Mexico

International Thomson Publishing GmbH
Königswinterer Strasse 418
53227 Bonn
Germany

International Thomson Publishing Asia
211 Henderson Road
#05-10 Henderson Building
Singapore 0315

International Thomson Publishing Japan
Hirakawacho Kyowa Building, 3F
2-2-1 Hirakawacho
Chiyoda-ku, Tokyo 102
Japan

Trademarks
Course Technology and the open book logo are registered trademarks and CourseKits is a trademark of Course Technology. Custom Editions and the I(T)P® logo are registered trademarks of International Thomson Publishing.

Microsoft, Windows, and Windows 95 are registered trademarks of Microsoft Corporation.
Netscape, Netscape Communications, Netscape Navigator, and the Netscape Communications logo are trademarks of Netscape Communications Corporation.

Some of the product names and company names used in this book have been used for identification purposes only and may be trademarks or registered trademarks of their respective manufacturers and sellers.

Disclaimer
Course Technology reserves the right to revise this publication and make changes from time to time in its content without notice.

ISBN 0-7600-4737-5

Printed in the United States of America

10 9 8 7 6 5 4 3 2

Preface The New Perspectives Series

What is the New Perspectives Series?

Course Technology's **New Perspectives Series** is an integrated system of instruction that combines text and technology products to teach computer concepts and micro-computer applications. Users consistently praise this series for innovative pedagogy, creativity, supportive and engaging style, accuracy, and use of interactive technology. The first New Perspectives text was published in January of 1993. Since then, the series has grown to more than 100 titles and has become the best-selling series on computer concepts and microcomputer applications. Others have imitated the New Perspectives features, design, and technologies, but none have replicated its quality and its ability to consistently anticipate and meet the needs of instructors and students.

How does this book I'm holding fit into the New Perspectives Series?

New Perspectives applications books are available in the following categories:

Brief books are typically about 150 pages long and are intended to teach only the essentials. They contain 2 to 4 tutorials. A Brief book is designed for a short course or for a one-term course, used in combination with other Brief books. The book you are holding is a Brief book.

Introductory books are typically about 300 pages long and consist of all 6 to 7 of the tutorials in the Brief book, plus 2 or 3 more tutorials that go beyond the basics.

Comprehensive books are typically about 600 pages long and consist of all of the tutorials in the Introductory books, plus 4 or 5 more Intermediate tutorials covering higher-level topics. Comprehensive books include Brief Windows tutorials, the Brief, Introductory and Intermediate tutorials, 3 or 4 Additional Cases, and a Reference Section.

Advanced books cover topics similar to those in the Comprehensive books, but in more depth. Advanced books present the most high-level coverage in the series.

Custom Books The New Perspectives Series offers you two ways to customize a New Perspectives text to fit your course exactly: *CourseKits*™, two or more texts pack-aged together in a box, and *Custom Editions*®, your choice of books bound together. Custom Editions offer you unparalleled flexibility in designing your concepts and applications courses. You can build your own book by ordering a combination of titles bound together to cover only the topics you want. Your students save because they buy only the materials they need. There is no minimum order, and books are spiral bound. Both CourseKits and Custom Editions offer significant price discounts. Contact your Course Technology sales representative for more information.

New Perspectives Series Microcomputer Applications

Brief Titles or Modules	Introductory Titles or Modules	Intermediate Modules	Advanced Titles or Modules	Other Modules
Brief	**Introductory**	**Comprehensive**	**Advanced**	**Custom Editions**
2 to 4 tutorials	Brief + 2 or 3 more tutorials	Introductory + 4 or 5 Intermediate tutorials + Brief Windows, Additional Cases and Reference section	Quick Review of basics + in-depth, high-level coverage	Choose from any of the above to build your own Custom Editions® or CourseKits™

How do the Windows 95 editions differ from the Windows 3.1 editions?

SESSION 1.2

Sessions   We've divided the tutorials into sessions. Each session is designed to be completed in about 45 minutes to an hour (depending, of course, upon student needs and the speed of your lab equipment). With sessions, learning is broken up into more easily-assimilated chunks. You can more accurately allocate time in your syllabus. Students can better manage the available lab time. Each session begins with a "session box," which quickly describes the skills students will learn in the session. Furthermore, each session is numbered, which makes it easier for you and your students to navigate and communicate about the tutorial. Look on page NG 5 for the session box that opens Session 1.1.

Quick Check

Quick Checks   Each session concludes with meaningful, conceptual Quick Check questions that test students' understanding of what they learned in the session. Answers to all of the Quick Check questions are at the back of the book preceding the Index. You can find examples of Quick Checks on pages NG 16 and NG 34.

New Design   We have retained the best of the old design to help students differentiate between what they are to *do* and what they are to *read*. The steps are clearly identified by their shaded background and numbered steps. Furthermore, this new design presents steps and screen shots in a larger, easier to read format. Some good examples of our new design are pages NG 102 and NG 119.

What features are retained in the Windows 95 editions of the New Perspectives Series?

"Read This Before You Begin" Page   This page is consistent with Course Technology's unequaled commitment to helping instructors introduce technology into the classroom. Technical considerations and assumptions about software are listed to help instructors save time and eliminate unnecessary aggravation. The "Read This Before You Begin" page for this book is on page NG 2.

Tutorial Case   Each tutorial begins with a problem presented in a case that is meaningful to students. The problem turns the task of learning how to use an application into a problem-solving process. The problems increase in complexity with each tutorial. These cases touch on multicultural, international, and ethical issues—so important to today's business curriculum. See page NG 3 for the case that begins Tutorial 1.

1.
2.
3.

Step-by-Step Methodology   This unique Course Technology methodology keeps students on track. They enter data, click buttons, or press keys always within the context of solving the problem posed in the tutorial case. The text constantly guides students, letting them know where they are in the course of solving the problem. In addition, the numerous screen shots include labels that direct students' attention to what they should look at on the screen. On almost every page in this book, you can find an example of how steps, screen shots, and labels work together.

TROUBLE?

TROUBLE? Paragraphs   These paragraphs anticipate the mistakes or problems that students are likely to have and help them recover and continue with the tutorial. By putting these paragraphs in the book, rather than in the Instructor's Manual, we facilitate independent learning and free the instructor to focus on substantive conceptual issues rather than on common procedural errors. Two representative examples of Trouble? are on pages NG 50 and NG 106.

Reference Windows   Reference Windows appear throughout the text. They are succinct summaries of the most important tasks covered in the tutorials. Reference Windows are specially designed and written so students can refer to them when doing the Tutorial Assignments and Case Problems, and after completing the course. Page NG 88 contains the Reference Window for creating hypertext links.

Task Reference   The Task Reference contains a summary of how to perform common tasks using the most efficient method, as well as references to pages where the task is discussed in more detail. It appears as a table at the end of the book. In this book the Task Reference is on pages NG 165-168.

Tutorial Assignments, Case Problems, and Lab Assignments   Each tutorial concludes with Tutorial Assignments, which provide students with additional hands-on practice of the skills they learned in the tutorial. The Tutorial Assignments are followed by four Case Problems that have approximately the same scope as the tutorial case. In the Windows 95 applications texts, there is always one Case Problem in the book and one in the Instructor's Manual that require students to solve the problem independently, either "from scratch" or with minimum guidance. Finally, if a Course Lab (see next page) accompanies the tutorial, Lab Assignments are included. Look on page NG 153 for the Tutorial Assignments for Tutorial 4. See page NG 154 for examples of Case Problems. The Lab Assignments for Tutorial 1 are on page NG 44.

Exploration Exercises   The Windows environment allows students to learn by exploring and discovering what they can do. Exploration Exercises can be Tutorial Assignments or Case Problems that challenge students, encourage them to explore the capabilities of the program they are using, and extend their knowledge using the Help facility and other reference materials. Page NG 81 contains Exploration Exercises for Tutorial 2.

The New Perspectives Series is known for using technology to help instructors teach and to help students learn. The technology-based teaching and learning materials available with the New Perspectives Series are known as CourseTools. What CourseTools are available with this textbook?

Course On-Line
CourseLabs
Data Files
Solutions Files

Course Labs: Now, Concepts Come to Life   Computer skills and concepts come to life with the New Perspectives Course Labs—highly-interactive tutorials that combine illustrations, animation, digital images, and simulations. The Labs guide students step-by-step, present them with Quick Check questions, let them explore on their own, test their comprehension, and provide printed feedback. A Lab Assignment is also included with this textbook. The Lab available with this book and the tutorial in which it appears is:

The Internet
World Wide Web   **E-Mail**
Tutorial 1

Course Online: A Website Dedicated to Keeping You and Your Students Up-To-Date
When you use a New Perspectives product, you can access Course Technology's faculty and student sites on the World Wide Web. You can browse the password-protected faculty online companions to obtain online Instructor's Manuals, Solution Files, Student Files, and more. Please see your Instructor's Manual or call your Course Technology customer service representative for more information. Students may access their online companions in the Student Center using the URL **http://coursetools.com**.

What additional supplements are available with this textbook?

Student Files Student Files contain all of the data that students will use to complete the tutorials, Tutorial Assignments, Case Problems and Additional Cases. A Readme file includes technical tips for lab management. See the inside covers of this book and the "Read This Before You Begin" page before Tutorial 1 for more information on Student Files.

The following supplements are included in the Review Pack that accompanies this textbook:

You will receive the following items in the Instructor's Resource Kit:
- Student Files
- The Internet: World Wide Web Lab
- E-mail Lab

Some of the supplements listed above are also available over the World Wide Web through Course Technology's password-protected faculty online companions. Please see your instructor's manual or call your Course Technology customer service representative for more information.

Acknowledgments

Thanks to Mac Mendelsohn for his encouragement and enthusiasm for this project and his support as it moved through multiple betas. Special thanks to Greg Bigelow's quality assurance team, especially Brian McCooey, whose eagle eye saved the day more than once. Thanks to the skills of production editor Christine Spillett and her team—Marie McCooey, Susan Gall, and Cristina Haley—this book took a smooth ride through production. Finally, thanks to my wife, Joan Carey, who served as this book's product manager and development editor. She was instrumental in getting the book finished as well as keeping me and the kiddies (Michael, Peter, Thomas, and John Paul) sane.

Patrick M. Carey

Table of **Contents**

NEW
PERSPECTIVES
S E R I E S

Creating Web Pages with Netscape™ Navigator Gold Software

BRIEF

TUTORIALS

Read This **Before You Begin**

TO THE STUDENT

STUDENT DISK

To complete the tutorials, Tutorial Assignments, and Case Problems in this book, you need a Student Disk. Your instructor will either provide you with a Student Disk or ask you to make your own.

If you are supposed to make your own Student Disk, you will need one blank, formatted high-density disk. You will need to copy a set of folders from a file server or standalone computer onto your disk. Your instructor will tell you which computer, drive letter, and folders contain the files you need.

COURSE LABS

This book features an interactive Course Lab to help you understand Internet World Wide Web concepts. There is a Lab Assignment at the end of Tutorial 1 that relates to this Lab. To start the Lab, click the **Start** button on the Windows 95 Taskbar, point to **Programs**, point to **Course Labs**, point to **New Perspectives Applications**, and click **Internet World Wide Web**.

USING YOUR OWN COMPUTER

If you are going to work through this book using your own computer, you need:

■ **Computer System** A system with Netscape Navigator Gold 3.0 browser and a connection to the internet.

■ **Student Disk** Ask your instructor or lab manager for details on how to get the Student Disk. You will not be able to complete the tutorials or exercises in this book using your own computer until you have a Student Disk. The student files may also be obtained electronically over the Internet. See the inside front or inside back cover of this book for more details.

■ **Course Lab** See your instructor or technical support person to obtain the Course Lab for use on your own computer.

VISIT OUR WORLD WIDE WEB SITE

Additional materials designed especially for you are available on the World Wide Web. Go to **http://coursetools.com**.

TO THE INSTRUCTOR

To complete the tutorials in this book, your students must use a set of student files. These files are stored on the Review Pack. Follow the instructions on the CD-ROM label and in the Readme file to copy them to your server or standalone computer. You can view the Readme file using WordPad.

Once the files are copied, you can make the Student Disk for the students yourself, or tell students where to find the files so they can make their own Student Disk.

COURSE LAB SOFTWARE

Tutorial 1 features an online, interactive Course Lab that introduces basic Internet World Wide Web concepts. This software is distributed on the Instructor's Resource Kit. To install the Lab software, follow the setup instructions on the CD-ROM label and in the Readme file. Once you have installed the Course Lab software, your students can start the Lab following the instructions in the Course Lab section above.

CTI SOFTWARE AND STUDENT FILES

You are granted a license to copy the Student Files and Course Lab to any computer or computer network used by students who have purchased this book. The Student Files are included in the Review Pack and may also be obtained electronically over the Internet. See the inside front or inside back cover of this book for more details.

Getting Started with Netscape Navigator Gold

Learning Netscape Navigator Fundamentals

In this tutorial you will:

- Review the structure of the Internet and the World Wide Web

- Start Netscape Navigator Gold

- Navigate the World Wide Web

- Create a simple Web page using the Netscape Page Wizard

- Add text to a Web page

- Add links, including an e-mail link, to a Web page

- Select design elements, such as colors, background patterns, and bullet and line styles

- Modify a Web page using the Netscape Editor

- Get help

West Concord Public Library

CASE The West Concord Public Library in central Minnesota has recently connected its network to the Internet. Muriel Bennett, the library's Information Sciences specialist, has hired you as a summer intern to assist in taking advantage of the new connection. Muriel sees two purposes for the Internet connection: to make information about the library and its services available to people in remote areas and to give library patrons the ability to tap into information sources at other libraries and institutions.

The library has a tight budget, however, and Muriel can't spend a lot of money training people how to use the Internet. She wants a system that will be easy to use with a minimum of instruction. Muriel knows that one of the most important developments on the Internet in recent years is the **World Wide Web**, a collection of documents and files that are all linked together so that it is easy even for novices to find and retrieve information. One of the popular tools for accessing the Web is Netscape Communications Corporation's Netscape Navigator software. Muriel has had a recent version of this software, Netscape Navigator Gold, installed on all library computers. Your first task will be to familiarize yourself with how the World Wide Web and the Internet operate and to learn some of the fundamentals of using Netscape. Then Muriel plans to involve you in creating the library's own Web document.

LAB

**The Internet
World Wide Web**

Using the Tutorials Effectively

These tutorials will help you learn about using Netscape Navigator Gold version 3.0 to create Web pages. The tutorials are designed to be used at a computer. Each tutorial is divided into sessions. Watch for the session headings, such as Session 1.1 and Session 1.2. Each session is designed to be completed in about 45 minutes, but take as much time as you need. It's also a good idea to take a break between sessions.

Before you begin, read the following questions and answers. They are designed to help you use the tutorials effectively.

Where do I start?

Each tutorial begins with a case, which sets the scene for the tutorial and gives you background information to help you understand what you will be doing in the tutorial. Read the case before you go to the lab. In the lab, begin with the first session of the tutorial.

How do I know what to do on the computer?

Each session contains steps that you will perform on the computer to learn how to use Netscape Navigator Gold to create Web pages. Read the text that introduces each series of steps. The steps you need to do at a computer are numbered and are set against a colored background. Read each step carefully and completely before you try it.

How do I know if I did the step correctly?

As you work, compare your computer screen with the corresponding figure in the tutorial. Don't worry if your screen display is somewhat different from the figure. The important parts of the screen display are labeled in each figure. Check to make sure these parts are on your screen.

What if I make a mistake?

Don't worry about making mistakes—they are part of the learning process. Paragraphs labeled "TROUBLE?" identify common problems and explain how to get back on track. Follow the steps in a TROUBLE? paragraph *only* if you are having the problem described. If you run into other problems:

- Carefully consider the current state of your system, the position of the pointer, and any messages on the screen.

- Complete the sentence, "Now I want to... ." Be specific, because you are identifying your goal.

- Develop a plan for accomplishing your goal, and put your plan into action.

How do I use the Reference Windows?

Reference Windows summarize the procedures you learn in the tutorial steps. Do not complete the actions in the Reference Windows when you are working through the tutorial. Instead, refer to the Reference Windows while you are working on the assignments at the end of the tutorial.

How can I test my understanding of the material I learned in the tutorial?

At the end of each session, you can answer the Quick Check questions. The answers for the Quick Checks are at the end of the book.

After you have completed the entire tutorial, you should complete the Tutorial Assignments. The Tutorial Assignments are carefully structured so you will review what you have learned and then apply your knowledge to new situations.

What if I can't remember how to do something?

You should refer to the Task Reference at the end of the book; it summarizes how to accomplish commonly performed tasks.

What are the Interactive Labs, and how should I use them?

Interactive Labs help you review concepts and practice skills that you learn in the tutorial. Lab icons at the beginning and in the margins of the tutorials indicate topics that have corresponding Labs. The Lab Assignments section includes instructions for how to use each Lab.

Now that you've seen how to use the tutorials effectively, you are ready to begin.

SESSION

1.1

In this session you will learn what the Internet is and how it operates. You will be introduced to the World Wide Web and will learn some of the basic principles of how the Web functions. Finally, you'll learn how to explore the Web using the Netscape Navigator Gold.

The World Wide Web

In the last few years the World Wide Web has quickly become the most popular way for computer users to share information. Many companies and organizations have seized upon this popularity to advertise their products on the Web. Private computer owners are using the Web to share their interests and talents with others. Various government agencies also see the Web as a useful tool for presenting information to citizens and making it easier to interact with their agencies. Now that the West Concord Public Library has Internet access, Muriel wants to explore ways to use the Web to benefit the library and its patrons. Muriel knows that you are eager to learn more about how the Web can help organizations operate effectively, so she decides to spend the first day of your summer internship giving you an overview of the structure of the Internet, the World Wide Web, and the tool you'll use most as you work on the Web: Netscape Navigator Gold.

The Structure of the Internet

Muriel begins by explaining that when computers are linked together so that they can exchange information and resources, they create a structure known as a **network**. Networks facilitate the sharing of files or programs among several users. They also allow one device, such as a printer, to serve the needs of several computers. One common network is the **Local Area Network**, or **LAN**, which usually involves linking computers that are located in a central place, such as an office building or a campus computer lab. This is the network structure the West Concord Public Library uses. Figure 1-1 shows an example of a LAN with only a handful of computers and a single shared printer. The library also has a **server**, a computer that stores computer files and makes them available to other computers on the network.

Figure 1-1 ◄
A local area
network

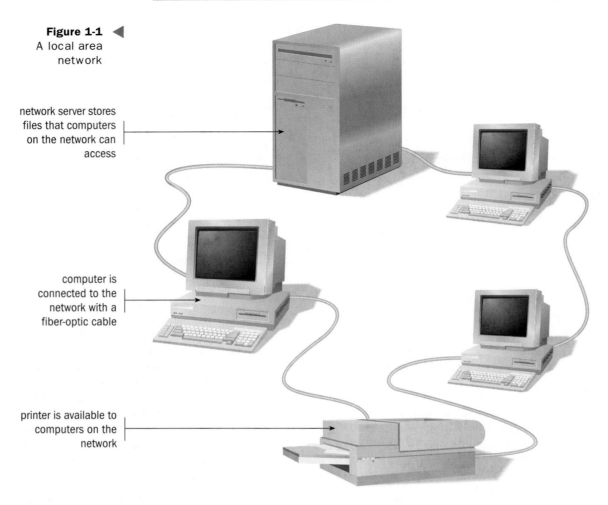

network server stores
files that computers
on the network can
access

computer is
connected to the
network with a
fiber-optic cable

printer is available to
computers on the
network

Networks can also be connected to each other to allow information to be shared between computers in different networks. The biggest and most famous example of this is the Internet, which is sometimes referred to as the "network of networks." The **Internet** is made up of millions of computers linked in networks all over the world. These networks communicate using standard rules of communication called **protocols**. The various networks and computers exchange information using fiber-optic cables, satellites, phone lines, infrared signals, and other telecommunications systems, as shown in Figure 1-2. Any user whose computer can be linked to a network that has Internet access can be a part of the worldwide Internet community.

Figure 1-2 ◀
Structure of
the Internet

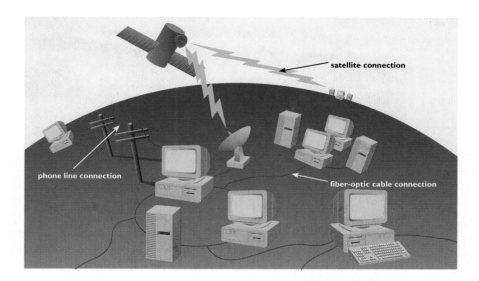

The Internet, by design, is a decentralized structure. Thus the Internet is fundamentally different from online services like CompuServe or America Online, which are organizations that retrieve, organize, and provide their subscribers quick and easy access to controlled information. In contrast, there is no Internet "company." Instead, the Internet is a collection of different organizations, such as universities and companies, that organize their own information resources in whatever way they want. The Internet is similar to the vast collection of information resources available in your community. You have access to libraries, bookstores, magazine racks, newspapers, and the television news, and no one controls all those different resources. Now imagine trying to find out all you can about, for example, the ozone layer. You might go to all the libraries and bookstores in your town without being sure what each has to offer until you get there. Finding information on the Internet can be a little like that. In time you learn which sites are good for different topics, and you develop a list of your own personal favorite Internet sites.

Even though the lack of central control can make it hard for beginners to "find their way" through the resources of the Internet, there are some advantages. The Internet is open to innovation and rapid growth as different organizations and individuals have the freedom to test new products and services and make them quickly available to Internet users. One such service developed in recent years is the World Wide Web.

The Structure of the World Wide Web

The foundation of the World Wide Web was laid in 1989 by Timothy Berners-Lee and other researchers at the CERN research facility near Geneva, Switzerland. They wanted to create an information system that would make it easy for researchers to share data and that required minimal training and support. They did this through a system of hypertext documents. A **hypertext document** is an electronic file that contains elements known as **links** that you can select, usually by clicking a mouse, to move to another part of the document or to another document entirely.

Hypertext is an efficient way of accessing information. When you read a book you follow a linear progression, reading one page after another. With hypertext, you progress through the pages in whatever way you want. Hypertext allows you to skip from one topic to another, following the information path that interests you. Figure 1-3 shows how topics might be organized in both a linear and hypertext model.

Figure 1-3 ◀
Linear vs.
Hypertext
documents

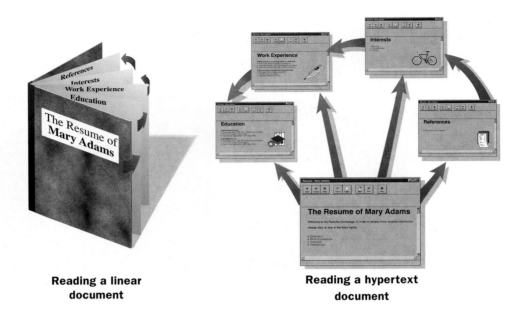

**Reading a linear
document**

**Reading a hypertext
document**

Hypertext appeals to researchers because they could include instructions for using hypertext within the hypertext document itself. The system not only gives you the information you need, it also tells you how to get it.

The system of hypertext documents developed at CERN proved to be easily adaptable to other information sources on the Internet. Within the space of a few years, hypertext documents were being created by several organizations for a large variety of topics. Because it was easy to link these different hypertext documents together, a single user could jump from one set of hypertext documents to another without much effort. This interconnected structure of hypertext documents became known as the World Wide Web or simply the Web.

Each hypertext document on the Web is called a **Web page**. A Web page can contain links to other Web pages located anywhere on the Internet—on the same computer as the original Web page or on an entirely different computer halfway across the world. The ability to cross-reference other Web pages with links is one of the most important features of the Web. Consider the ozone example. You would find your search for information on the ozone layer considerably simplified if each library, bookstore, or newspaper contained cross-references to the materials that each of the other sources offered.

In addition to offering access to other Web pages, links can also connect you to many other document types. Clicking a link might access a scanned photograph or a file containing sound or video clips. A link could lead you into forums where users share information on topics of common interest. The link might even point to the e-mail address of a particular individual so that you can send a message. You can access just about any piece of information available on the Internet through a hypertext link.

In the end, perhaps the greatest source of the Web's popularity lies in the ease with which users can create their own Web pages. All you need is an account on a computer connected to the Internet that allows you to store your Web page and make it available for others to read. This is in marked contrast to other Internet services, which often required the expertise of the computer systems manager to set up and maintain. Many universities now give students the opportunity of creating their own Web pages, and companies that sell access to the Internet, called **Internet Service Providers** or **ISPs**, include Web pages as part of their standard packages to subscribers.

These factors have contributed to the unprecedented growth of the World Wide Web. Figure 1-4 shows that in 1993 there were only several hundred Web sites worldwide. By the beginning of 1996 there were almost 100,000 such sites. The number of sites is doubling at a rate of once every 5 months (these estimates come from Matthew Gray of net.Genesis Corporation). Is there any doubt why the West Concord Public Library sees the Web as an important information tool for its patrons?

Figure 1-4 ◀
Growth of the
World Wide
Web

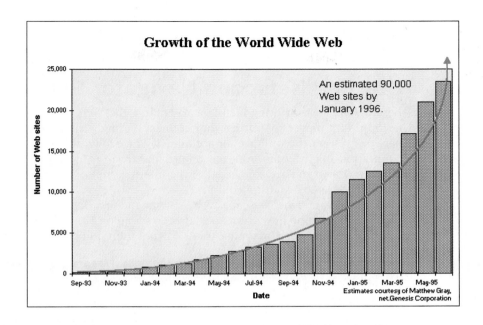

Web Servers and Web Browsers

Muriel explains that when a user tries to view a Web page there are two components involved. As shown in Figure 1-5, one component is the **Web server,** the computer that stores the document that the user accesses. The second is the **Web browser,** the software program on the user's computer that retrieves the document from the Web server and displays its contents on the user's computer. Browsers can be text-based—in which case they show only text—or they can be graphical—capable of displaying graphics, special fonts, and multimedia elements such as sound and video. Netscape Navigator Gold is an example of a graphical browser. In Figure 1-5, a browser in California is accessing a document stored on a Web server in Florida.

Figure 1-5 ◀
Using a browser
to view a Web
document on a
server

Netscape browser —

browser in California
locates and displays
document stored on
server in Florida

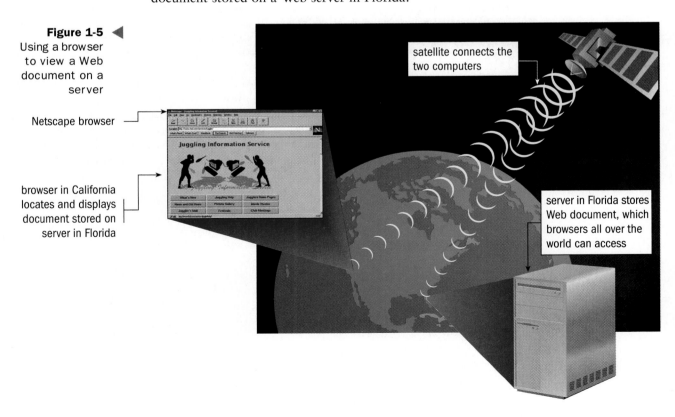

Muriel suggests that you connect to the Internet and start using Netscape to explore Web documents so you can get ideas for the West Concord Public Library Web page you'll be creating.

Starting Netscape Navigator Gold

Before you can start using Netscape to explore the Web, you must have an Internet connection. In a university setting your connection might come from the campus local area network on which you have an account. If you are working on a home computer, your connection might come over the phone line from an account with an Internet service provider. Once you are connected to the Internet, you can start Netscape using whatever method your site has installed.

When you start the Netscape Web browser, the first Web page you see is called the **home page**. Depending on how Netscape has been set up on your computer, you computer might display the Netscape Communications Corporation home page, shown in Figure 1-6.

Figure 1-6 ◀
Netscape
home page

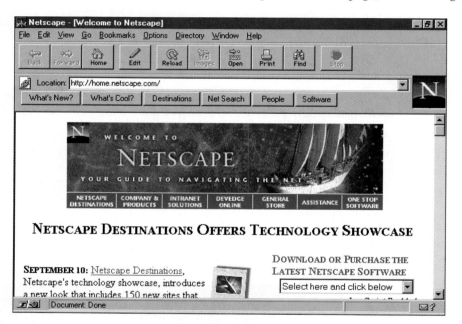

The term "home page" also can refer to the Web page that a person, organization, or business has created to give information about itself. For example, Netscape Communications Corporation's home page provides fundamental information about Netscape and its software. At the West Concord Public Library, the home page that appears is that of SELCO, the organization of libraries in Southeastern Minnesota. In Session 1.2, you will begin creating a home page for the West Concord Public Library so it has its own and doesn't have to use the SELCO home page. The home page that appears on a university's computer might be a page designed by and for the university.

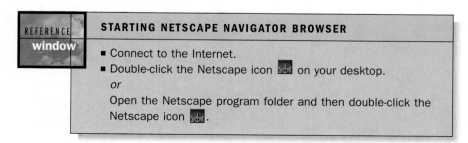

REFERENCE
window

STARTING NETSCAPE NAVIGATOR BROWSER

- Connect to the Internet.
- Double-click the Netscape icon 🖳 on your desktop.
  or
  Open the Netscape program folder and then double-click the Netscape icon 🖳.

The West Concord Public Library accesses the Internet via an account with a local Internet Service Provider. Muriel gives you the library's Internet account information and instructions for accessing the account, and you are ready to begin.

To start Netscape Navigator Gold:

1. Connect to your Internet account.

TROUBLE? If don't know how to connect to your Internet account, talk to your instructor or technical support person.

2. Double-click the **Netscape** icon , located either on your computer's desktop or within the Netscape program window. The Netscape window for the West Concord Public Library computer opens, displaying the Web page shown in Figure 1-7. Your home page will be different. For example, you might see the home page for your university or Internet Service Provider.

TROUBLE? If you can't locate the Netscape icon or the Netscape program folder, ask your instructor or technical support person for help.

Figure 1-7
SELCO home page

menu bar

toolbar; your buttons might look different

Location box

directory buttons

document window

status bar

activity indicator

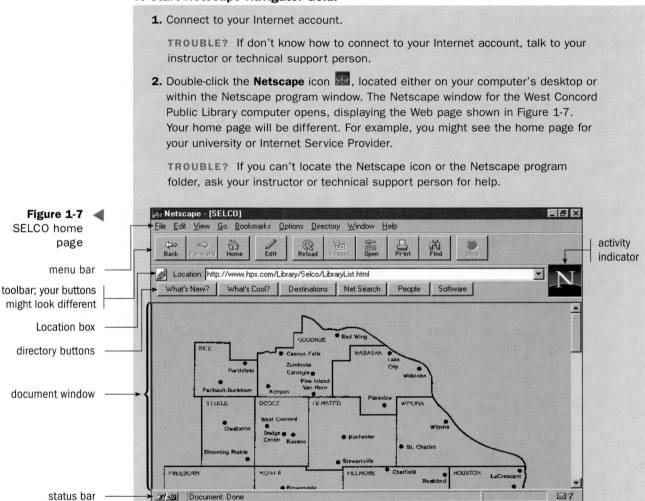

Regardless of which page appears when you first start Netscape, you should find that your window shares some common elements with the one displayed in Figure 1-7. Muriel suggests that before you try to navigate the World Wide Web, you examine some of the parts of the Netscape window, discussed in Figure 1-8.

Figure 1-8 ◀
Elements in
the Netscape
window

Window element	Description
Document window	Displays the contents of the current Web page.
Menu bar	Gives you access to Netscape commands, including commands to access popular Web pages and to configure how Netscape operates on your system.
Toolbar	Gives you access to the more common Netscape commands through a single mouse-click. The toolbar button will show either an icon representing the command, text representing the command, or both an icon and text, depending on how the software is configured.
Location box	Identifies the address of the Web page currently displayed in the Netscape window.
Directory buttons	Provide single-click access to several Web pages maintained by the Netscape Corporation.
Activity indicator	Displays the Netscape logo with comets streaking across the sky to tell you whether information you are retrieving is being properly transmitted. If the comets stop, you know there is a problem with the connection.
Status bar	Indicates how much of the Web document has been retrieved from the Web server.

Navigating the Internet

Once you are connected to the Internet and you have started the Netscape browser, you navigate the Web by moving from one Web page to another. The home page that appears when you first start Netscape will usually contain links to other pages. As discussed earlier, you can move from one Web page to another by clicking the links that interest you.

Links can appear in two ways: as text that you click or as a graphic that you click. A **text link** is a word or phrase that is underlined and often boldfaced or colored differently. Text links can represent pages that you haven't visited yet or pages that you have visited. The Netscape browser uses a different color for previously-visited pages. This feature makes it easy for you to retrace your steps as you try to locate pages that you've viewed in the past. The second type of link, the **graphic link**, is a graphic image that you click to jump to another location. When you move your mouse over a link, whether it is a text or graphic link, the pointer changes shape from � to ᕼ. The ᕼ pointer shape indicates that when you click, you will activate the link and jump to the new location.

Muriel suggests that you select a link that looks interesting and try jumping to its page.

To activate a hypertext link:

1. Scroll down the page in Netscape's document window until you see a text link, which is usually underlined and in a different color. Scrolling down the SELCO home page reveals a list of links to other libraries in the area. See Figure 1-9. Other home pages will show different links.

   TROUBLE? If you can't locate a link in the page you are viewing, ask your instructor or technical resource person for help.

2. Once you see a link that interests you, move your mouse pointer over the text until the shape of the pointer changes from � to ᕼ.

Figure 1-9
Pointing
at a link

underlined text in a
different color
indicates a link

pointer changes when
you point at a link

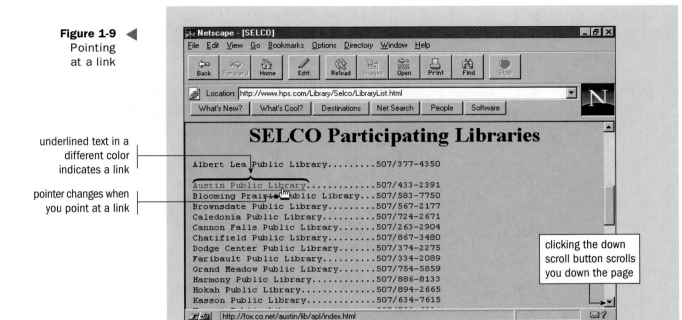

clicking the down
scroll button scrolls
you down the page

3. Click the link. Netscape retrieves the Web page referred to by the link. Figure 1-10 displays the Web page that is linked to the text, "Austin Public Library," from the SELCO home page. Your link will jump to a different page.

TROUBLE? If a new page does not appear on your screen, it might contain numerous graphics and therefore take longer to retrieve. Check the activity indicator and status bar to verify that Netscape is trying to access the page.

TROUBLE? If you receive an error message, acknowledge the message then try a different link on the page or talk to your instructor or computer support person. It's possible that the page you tried to access is no longer available or is located on a server that is busy.

Figure 1-10
Jumping to
a new page

you jump to a new
page; yours will
look different

Netscape "remembers" which pages you've been to during your current Web session. When you want to return to the Web page you were viewing prior to the current one, you can use the navigation buttons shown on the Netscape toolbar. There are three navigation buttons on the toolbar, discussed in Figure 1-11.

Figure 1-11 ◀
Navigation
buttons

Button	Icon	Description
Back	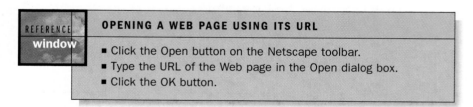	Returns you to the Web page you were most recently viewing. This button is active only when you have viewed more than one Web page in the current session.
Forward		Reverses the effect of the Back button, returning you to previously viewed pages.
Home		Takes you to your home page, the first page that the Netscape browser displays.

Muriel suggests that you use the Back button to return from the Austin Public Library page to the previous page, the SELCO home page.

To return to the previous page:

1. Click the **Back** button on the Netscape toolbar. Netscape opens the previous Web page—your home page.

Retrieving a Specific Web Page

Each page on the Web has a unique address called its **Uniform Resource Locator,** or more commonly, **URL.** If you know the URL of a Web page, you can go directly to that page rather than navigating through a series of hypertext links to reach it. Notice that the Netscape window shows the URL of the active Web page in the Location box. For example, in Figure 1-10, the URL for the Austin Public Library page is http://fox.co.net/austin/lib/apl/index.html. You'll learn how to interpret URLs such as this one in Tutorial 3.

REFERENCE window	**OPENING A WEB PAGE USING ITS URL**
	▪ Click the Open button on the Netscape toolbar.
	▪ Type the URL of the Web page in the Open dialog box.
	▪ Click the OK button.

One Web page that Muriel guesses West Concord Public Library patrons will request often is the Library of Congress home page. The URL for that page is http://www.loc.gov. Muriel asks you enter that URL to jump directly to that page.

To access the Library of Congress home page:

1. Click the **Open** button on the Netscape toolbar.

2. Type **http://www.loc.gov** in the Open Location box. Make sure you type the URL exactly as shown.

3. Verify that the **Open in Browser window** option button is selected. See Figure 1-12.

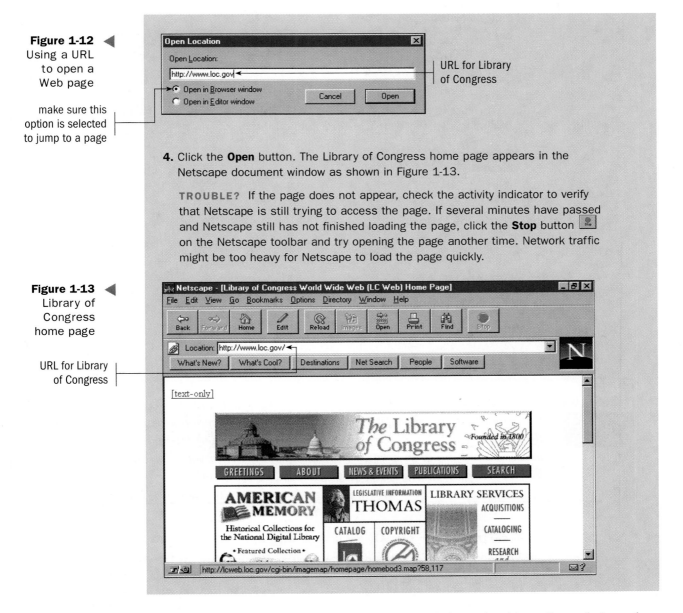

Figure 1-12
Using a URL
to open a
Web page

URL for Library
of Congress

make sure this
option is selected
to jump to a page

4. Click the **Open** button. The Library of Congress home page appears in the Netscape document window as shown in Figure 1-13.

TROUBLE? If the page does not appear, check the activity indicator to verify that Netscape is still trying to access the page. If several minutes have passed and Netscape still has not finished loading the page, click the **Stop** button on the Netscape toolbar and try opening the page another time. Network traffic might be too heavy for Netscape to load the page quickly.

Figure 1-13
Library of
Congress
home page

URL for Library
of Congress

Muriel suggests that you try navigating around the Web a bit until you feel comfortable using the Netscape navigation buttons and hypertext links. You can do that on your own, using whatever links are available on the pages you find. This book's focus is on creating Web pages, not navigating the Web. If you want more information about using Netscape and the Web, see *New Perspectives on Using the Internet with Netscape Navigator Software*, published by Course Technology.

Exiting Netscape

When you are ready to leave Netscape, you first close the Netscape program using the Exit option on the File menu or by clicking the Close button on the Netscape title bar. Then you need to disconnect from the Internet. The process of disconnecting from the Internet varies for different users and networks. Talk to your instructor or technical support person for the steps you need to follow in order to sever your Internet connection.

To close Netscape:

1. Click the **Close** button ☒.

2. Disconnect from the Internet.

Muriel tells you that after you take a short break, the two of you can begin planning a Web page for the West Concord Public Library.

Quick Check

1. What is a local area network?

2. What is the Internet?

3. Compare the structure of the Internet to an online service like CompuServe or America Online. How does the World Wide Web make the Internet more accessible to new users?

4. What are a Web browser and Web server?

5. What are hypertext links?

6. A home page is _____.

SESSION 1.2

In this session you will create a Web page using Netscape's Page Wizard. You'll learn about the common elements of a Web page and then implement them by going through the Page Wizard steps. You'll learn how to add links to your page, including an e-mail link, and then delete them. You'll then work on your page's appearance. You'll learn how to save a Web page and finally, how to print it.

Elements of a Web Page

When you return from your break, you and Muriel discuss the page she would like you to create for the West Concord Public Library. Creating a Web page involves planning both the content and the appearance. You can plan the content by asking questions like: What information do I want to convey? What links do I want to include?

Once you have settled on your content, you should plan your design. You can include colors, interesting fonts, a stylized background, graphics, and other design elements like lines and tables. Keep in mind, however, that a browser takes much longer to retrieve a Web page that contains a lot of graphics. If your page takes too long to retrieve, your target audience might lose patience and skip your page.

Muriel draws the sketch shown in Figure 1-14. You notice that the page Muriel envisions contains links to the Web pages of other libraries in Southeastern Minnesota.

Figure 1-14
Plan for West
Concord Public
Library home
page

title

description

links

e-mail link

lines

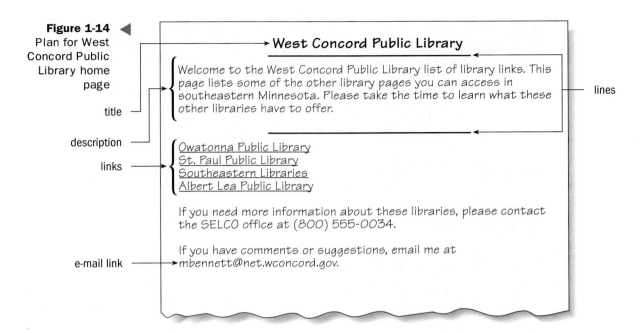

West Concord Public Library

Welcome to the West Concord Public Library list of library links. This page lists some of the other library pages you can access in southeastern Minnesota. Please take the time to learn what these other libraries have to offer.

Owatonna Public Library
St. Paul Public Library
Southeastern Libraries
Albert Lea Public Library

If you need more information about these libraries, please contact the SELCO office at (800) 555-0034.

If you have comments or suggestions, email me at mbennett@net.wconcord.gov.

The page that Muriel sketched contains the following elements:

- A page title.
- A description of the contents and purpose of the page.
- Links to other Web pages.
- A link to Muriel's e-mail address so that interested users can contact Muriel quickly and easily.
- Horizontal lines to divide the page into different sections to make it easier for patrons to read.

Using the Netscape Page Wizard

Muriel tells you that Netscape provides a tool to create simple Web pages called the **Netscape Page Wizard**. The Netscape Page Wizard is not a software program installed on your computer. Instead, it is a page on the World Wide Web, designed and maintained by Netscape Communications Corporation. However, you can access the Page Wizard from the Netscape menus. The Page Wizard walks you through the process of creating your page, prompting you for the content of the page, including a page heading, descriptive paragraph, and concluding text. You can also use the Page Wizard to create a list of hypertext links to other pages of interest. The Page Wizard provides options for controlling the appearance of your page including the page background.

You can work with the Page Wizard options in any order you want. When you have added or modified all the elements you want on your page, the Page Wizard uses that information to create a file that you can save to a folder on your computer and ultimately publish on the Web for other users to access.

Muriel suggests that you create the first version of the West Concord Public Library page using the Page Wizard. She'll then look over the page you created and suggest ways you can modify the page once you've created it.

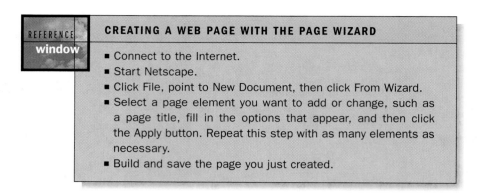

REFERENCE
window

CREATING A WEB PAGE WITH THE PAGE WIZARD

- Connect to the Internet.
- Start Netscape.
- Click File, point to New Document, then click From Wizard.
- Select a page element you want to add or change, such as a page title, fill in the options that appear, and then click the Apply button. Repeat this step with as many elements as necessary.
- Build and save the page you just created.

You decide to start the Page Wizard so you can begin creating a home page for the West Concord Public Library.

To start the Netscape Page Wizard:

1. Access your Internet account and start Netscape Navigator Gold.

2. Once your home page is loaded, click **File**, point to **New Document**, then click **From Wizard**. Netscape retrieves the Netscape Page Wizard page as shown in Figure 1-15.

   TROUBLE? If the Page Wizard doesn't appear, it might be temporarily unavailable. Try again later.

Figure 1-15 ◀
Netscape Page
Wizard

empty frames

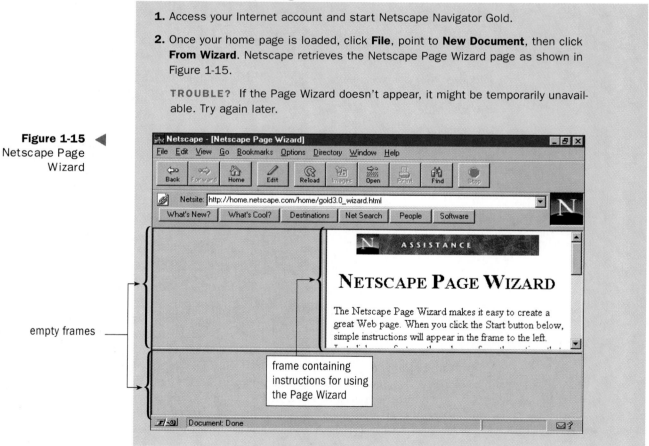

frame containing
instructions for using
the Page Wizard

Working with Page Wizard Frames

The Netscape Page Wizard shown in Figure 1-15 uses three frames. A **frame** is a section of the document window. Each frame can have its own set of scroll bars and can display the contents of a different Web page. When the Page Wizard opens, instructions for using the Page Wizard appear in the frame on the right side of the document window. The left and bottom frames are left empty. To create your page, you need to locate and then click the Page Wizard Start button, located at the bottom of the right frame.

To scroll the Page Wizard frame and start the Page Wizard:

1. Scroll to the bottom of the right frame until you locate the Start button. See Figure 1-16.

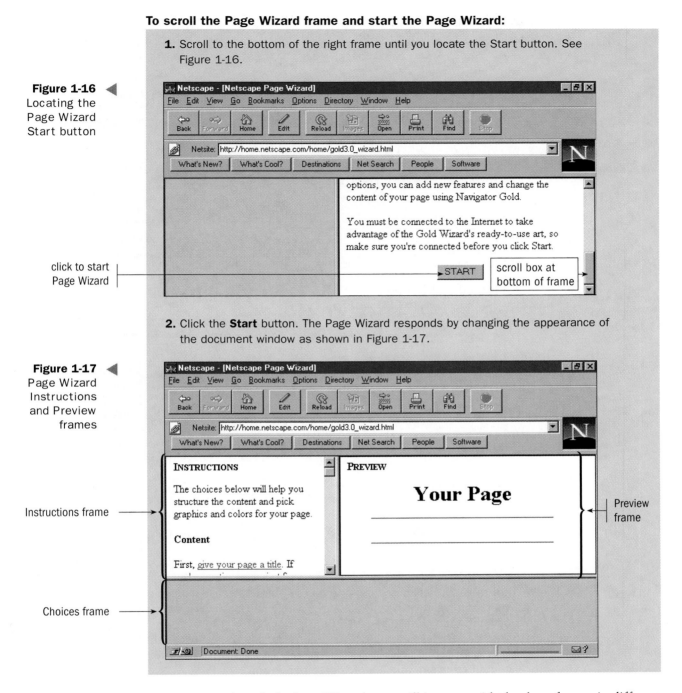

Figure 1-16 ◄
Locating the
Page Wizard
Start button

click to start |
Page Wizard |

options, you can add new features and change the content of your page using Navigator Gold.

You must be connected to the Internet to take advantage of the Gold Wizard's ready-to-use art, so make sure you're connected before you click Start.

→ START

scroll box at
bottom of frame

2. Click the **Start** button. The Page Wizard responds by changing the appearance of the document window as shown in Figure 1-17.

Figure 1-17 ◄
Page Wizard
Instructions
and Preview
frames

Instructions frame ——→

Choices frame ——→

INSTRUCTIONS

The choices below will help you structure the content and pick graphics and colors for your page.

Content

First, give your page a title. If

PREVIEW

Your Page

———————————

Preview
frame

Document: Done

As you work with the Page Wizard, you will interact with the three frames in different ways. The left frame is the **Instructions frame**, where the Page Wizard lists the elements of the page that you can create or change. Once you click an element from that frame, your options for that element appear in the **Choices frame**, the frame at the bottom of the screen. Right now the Choices frame is blank because you haven't selected a page element in the Instructions frame yet. When you click an element, such as the page title, the Choices frame will display the options you have for entering your page title. As you select and modify page elements, the Page Wizard displays a preview of your page in the right frame, the **Preview frame**.

At times you might find that the preset sizes of the frame don't meet your needs. You can enlarge or shrink a frame by dragging one of the frame borders up, down, to the left, or to the right. When you point at the horizontal border, for example, the pointer changes from ⬚ to ⬚, indicating that you are ready to drag. Try resizing one of the Page Wizard frames now.

To resize a frame:

1. Point at the top border of the lower frame. The mouse pointer changes from ⬚ to ⬚ .

2. Drag the border up about an inch. See Figure 1-18.

TROUBLE? To drag the border up, press and hold down the mouse button and then move the pointer. Release the mouse button when the border is where you want it.

Figure 1-18
Resizing
a frame

pointer changes when
you resize frame

frame border

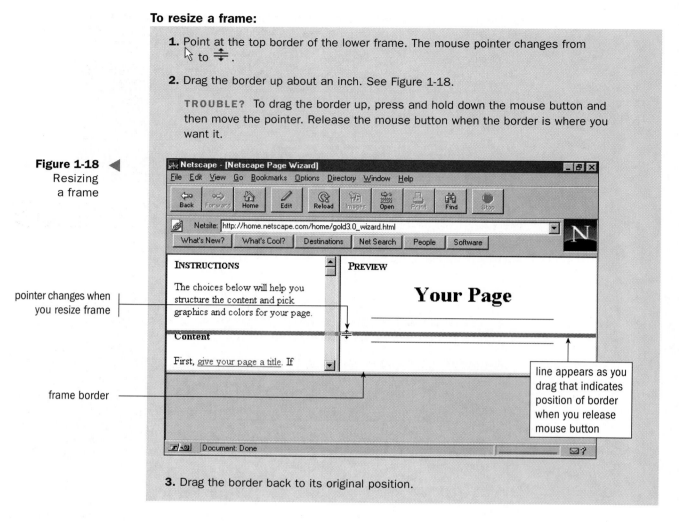

line appears as you drag that indicates position of border when you release mouse button

3. Drag the border back to its original position.

Entering Page Content with the Page Wizard

You can create your page by following the order of the elements listed in the Instructions box—enter the first element, then the second, and so on. But the Page Wizard is flexible. You can enter elements in any order you want, and if you decide you want to change an element you've already worked with, you just click that element again in the Instructions frame and then edit it as necessary.

You decide to enter all your page content first, then enter all the links, and finally work on the page design. You look back at your sketch to see that your content includes a title, a brief description, and a concluding paragraph.

When you select a text element to work with, such as a title, a box will appear in the Choices frame. This box will contain **prompt text** or text that tells you what to type. You must delete the prompt text and then enter your own text.

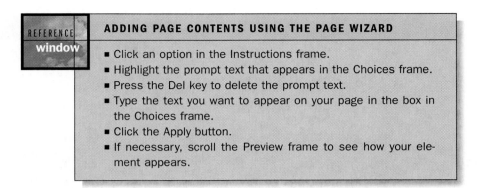

REFERENCE window

ADDING PAGE CONTENTS USING THE PAGE WIZARD

- Click an option in the Instructions frame.
- Highlight the prompt text that appears in the Choices frame.
- Press the Del key to delete the prompt text.
- Type the text you want to appear on your page in the box in the Choices frame.
- Click the Apply button.
- If necessary, scroll the Preview frame to see how your element appears.

Entering a Page Title

You decide to begin by entering a title. You'll use the name of the library as the title for the home page.

To add a title to your Web page:

1. Click the **give your page a title** link in the Instructions frame. A box appears in the Choices frame at the bottom of the Page Wizard window. Notice that the link changes color, indicating that you've accessed this link. The different color helps you keep track of what links you've used so far.

2. Highlight the prompt in the Title box, **Type your title here.**

3. Press the **Del** key to delete the prompt in the Title box.

   TROUBLE? This key might say Delete on your keyboard.

4. Type **West Concord Library** in the Title box.

   TROUBLE? If you make a typing error, press the Backspace key to delete what you typed, then retype the entry correctly.

5. Click the **Apply** button. The title you entered appears in the Preview frame as shown in Figure 1-19.

Figure 1-19 ◀
Entering a title

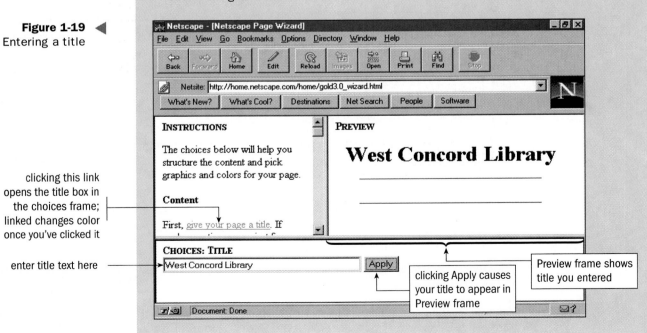

clicking this link opens the title box in the choices frame; linked changes color once you've clicked it

enter title text here

clicking Apply causes your title to appear in Preview frame

Preview frame shows title you entered

Entering Introductory Text

Most Web pages have a paragraph just below the title that serves as an introduction to the page. This text can describe the page, its goals, and its resources, or it can give brief instructions about how the page operates. You decide to add a paragraph that gives instructions about using the West Concord Public Library page.

To add an introduction to your Web page:

1. Scroll down the Instructions frame until you see the "type an introduction" link.

2. Click the **type an introduction** link in the Instructions frame. A box with a vertical scrollbar appears in the Choices frame.

   TROUBLE? If the bottom frame needs more space to display the text you are about to enter, you can change the size of the frame by moving the frame border up.

3. Highlight the prompt in the box, **Type your introduction here**, in the Choices frame, then press the **Del** key.

4. Type the following paragraph into the box in the Choices frame. As you type, the text will scroll up and seem to disappear. Don't worry. You can use the vertical scroll arrows to see the text you typed.

   Welcome to the West Concord Public Library list of library links. This page lists some of the other library pages you can access in Southeastern Minnesota. Please take the time to learn what these other libraries have to offer.

5. Click the **Apply** button. The Preview frame now shows your introductory text. See Figure 1-20.

Figure 1-20 ◀
Entering introductory text

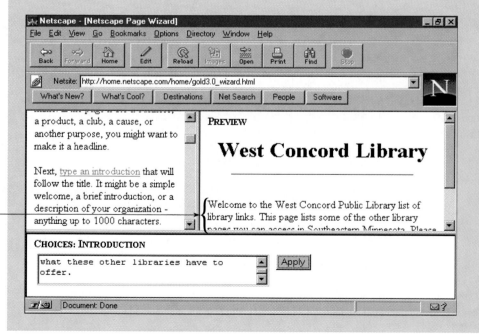

introductory text

Entering a Closing Paragraph

The Netscape Page Wizard allows you to add a closing paragraph to your page that you can use for directions, comments, or your favorite quotes. You'll have to scroll down the Instructions frame to locate the link that helps you add a closing paragraph.

You decide to add a few sentences telling patrons where they can go to get more help as your closing paragraph.

To add a closing paragraph to the Web page:

1. Scroll down the Instructions frame, then click the **type a paragraph of text to serve as a conclusion** link.

2. Highlight the prompt, **Type your conclusion here**, in the Choices frame then press the **Del** key.

3. Type **If you need more information about these libraries, please contact the SELCO office at (800) 555-0034.** in the Conclusion box.

4. Click the **Apply** button.

5. Scroll to see how the Preview frame changes to show your concluding paragraph. See Figure 1-21.

Figure 1-21 ◀
Entering a
concluding
paragraph

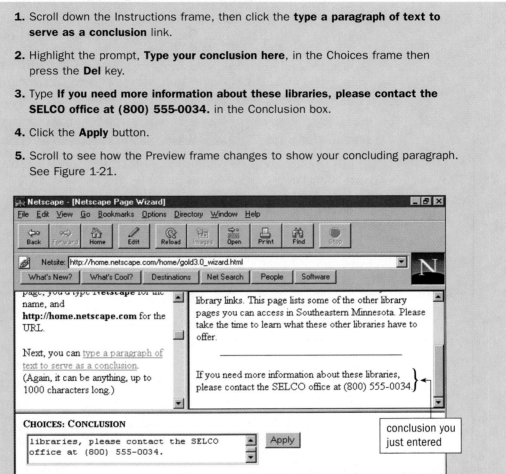

Correcting a Mistake

When you look at your notes you notice that you and Muriel agreed the title of the page would be West Concord Public Library, not West Concord Library. You'll need to correct this error by reselecting the page element that needs correcting. When you select that element from the Instructions frame, the Choices frame displays the current entry for that element.

To correct the title:

1. Click the **give your page a title** link in the Instructions frame (you might have to scroll up to see it).

2. Move the mouse pointer between the words "Concord" and "Library" in the Title box in the Choices frame and then click.

3. Change the text to **West Concord Public Library** then click the **Apply** button. The title should now be updated in the Preview frame.

Adding and Removing Links

After adding the page title, introductory paragraph, and conclusion, you next decide to enter the hypertext links. The Netscape Page Wizard makes it easy for you to add links to your page, but be aware that you are limited by the Page Wizard to no more than four hypertext links. When you add a link, the Page Wizard displays two boxes in the Choices frame: one for the text you'd like to use to describe the link, and one for the URL of the link itself. When entering a URL you should pay close attention to the case of each letter. Some pages will not load if you substitute a lowercase letter for an uppercase letter. If you want to add more links than the four allowed by the Page Wizard, you'll need to edit your page, using techniques you'll learn later in this book.

Adding a Link

Muriel has already given you the names and URLs for four nearby libraries that have their own home pages that she wants placed in this list.

To create a list of links:

1. Locate and then click the **add some hot links to other Web pages** link in the Instructions frame.

   The Choices frame now prompts you for the name of the link that you want to create and the link's URL.

2. Highlight the prompt in the Name box, **Type the name of your hot link here**, then press the **Del** key. The first link you'll add will be for the Owattona Public Library page.

3. Type **Owatonna Public Library** in the Name box then press the **Tab** key.

4. Highlight the prompt in the box, **http://your.url/goes/here.html**, then press the **Del** key.

5. Type **http://www.ic.owatonna.mn.us/lib** in the URL box. Make sure you type the URL accurately. Your new entry should look like Figure 1-22.

Figure 1-22 ◀
Entering a link

choices that appear
when you add links

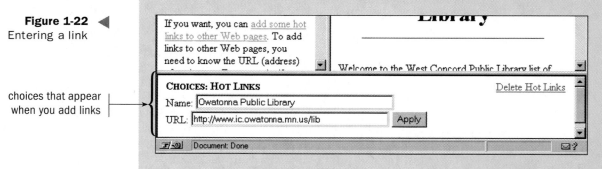

6. Click the **Apply** button. After a few seconds, the link appears in the Preview frame as shown in Figure 1-23 (you might have to scroll down to see it). Notice the "Hot Links" heading that Netscape automatically includes. You'll want to change this later.

   TROUBLE? Creating and placing the link might take your browser several seconds. Do not worry if the Preview frame doesn't change immediately.

Figure 1-23 ◄
Link in Preview
frame

first link; appears in
different color

Choices frame is
ready for you to
enter next link

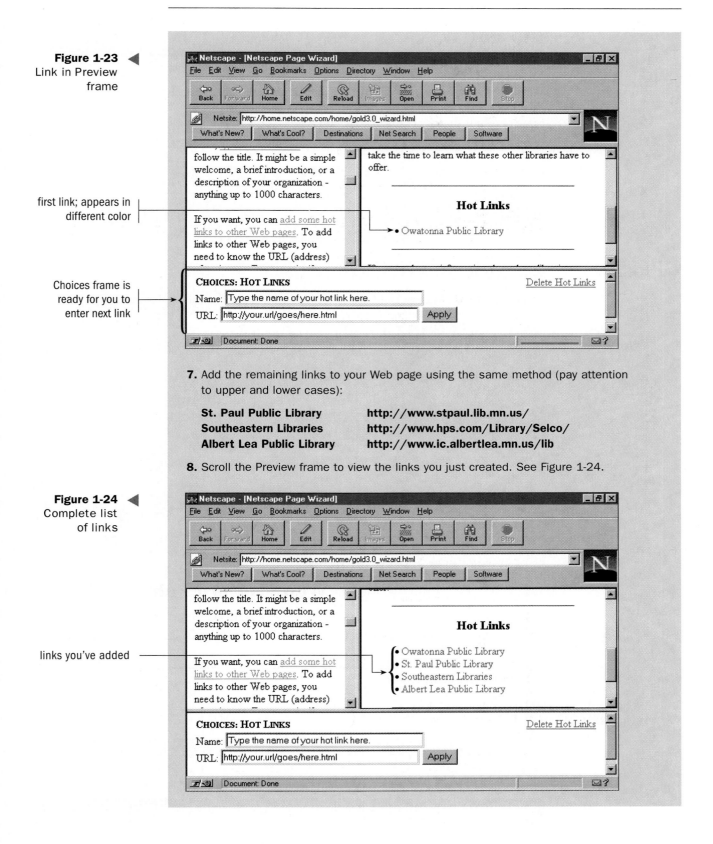

7. Add the remaining links to your Web page using the same method (pay attention to upper and lower cases):

St. Paul Public Library   **http://www.stpaul.lib.mn.us/**
Southeastern Libraries   **http://www.hps.com/Library/Selco/**
Albert Lea Public Library   **http://www.ic.albertlea.mn.us/lib**

8. Scroll the Preview frame to view the links you just created. See Figure 1-24.

Figure 1-24 ◄
Complete list
of links

links you've added

Removing a Link

Muriel stops by to observe your work and tells you that the Albert Lea Public Library Web page is still under construction and is not available to users. She decides that you should remove it from the list for now. The Netscape Page Wizard makes it easy to remove a link that you created. As you added links to the page, it stored those links in a list. You can access this list to remove one or more links.

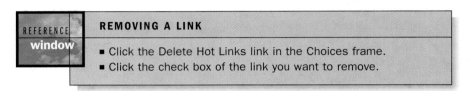

REFERENCE window	**REMOVING A LINK**
	■ Click the Delete Hot Links link in the Choices frame.
	■ Click the check box of the link you want to remove.

To remove the Albert Lea Public Library link:

1. Click the **Delete Hot Links** link in the Choices frame. The list of links appears in the Choices frame, preceded by check boxes.

   TROUBLE? If you can't see the entire list, either enlarge the Choices frame or scroll down it.

2. Click the check box for the Albert Lea Public Library link. The link is removed from the list. Your Preview frame should appear as shown in Figure 1-25.

   TROUBLE? If you can't see the links, scroll down the Preview frame until you can.

Figure 1-25 ◀
Deleting a link

clicking a check box
removes link
from page

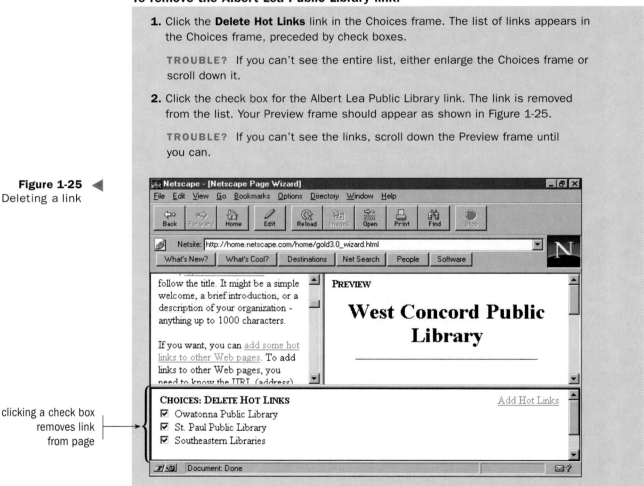

Adding an E-mail Link

Muriel has indicated that she would like to be listed as the contact person for the West Concord Public Library Web page. She wants you to insert a link to her e-mail address in the page so patrons viewing the page can e-mail her directly. The Page Wizard includes an option for creating a link to an e-mail address in the Instructions frame. Muriel's e-mail address is mbennett@net.wconcord.gov.

To add a link to Muriel's e-mail address:

1. Locate and then click the **add an e-mail link** in the Instructions frame. The Choices frame displays a text box for entering e-mail addresses.

2. Highlight the prompt, **yourname@yourhost.yourdomain.com**, in the Choices frame then press the **Del** key.

3. Type **mbennett@net.wconcord.gov** in the E-mail link box.

4. Click the **Apply** button.

5. Scroll down the Preview frame to see Muriel's e-mail address, shown in Figure 1-26. Users will be able to send mail to Muriel by clicking the link (assuming that the user's browser supports links to e-mail addresses—not all browsers do).

Figure 1-26 ◄
E-mail link

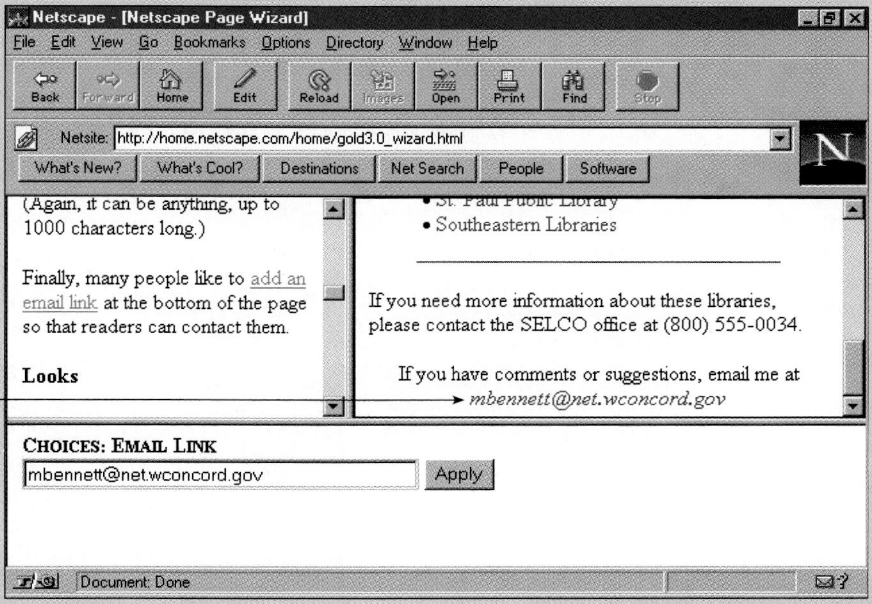

Muriel's e-mail
address

Designing Your Page

After completing the entry of your text elements and hypertext links, you are ready to start working on the page's appearance. The Page Wizard allows you to choose different colors for different elements, including:

- page background
- text
- linked text
- previously visited linked text

You can specify the color of each page element individually, or you can use one of the Page Wizard's preset color combinations that applies each page element color for you.

Selecting a Preset Color Combination

Using a preset color combination will save you time, but the end result may not be exactly what you want. You decide to start with one of the Page Wizard's anyway, knowing that you can modify each particular element afterward.

To use a preset color combination:

1. Scroll down the Instructions frame and click the **a preset color combination** link. A list of color combinations appears in the bottom frame as displayed in Figure 1-27.

Figure 1-27 ◀
Available color
combinations

preset color
combinations

you'll apply this
combination

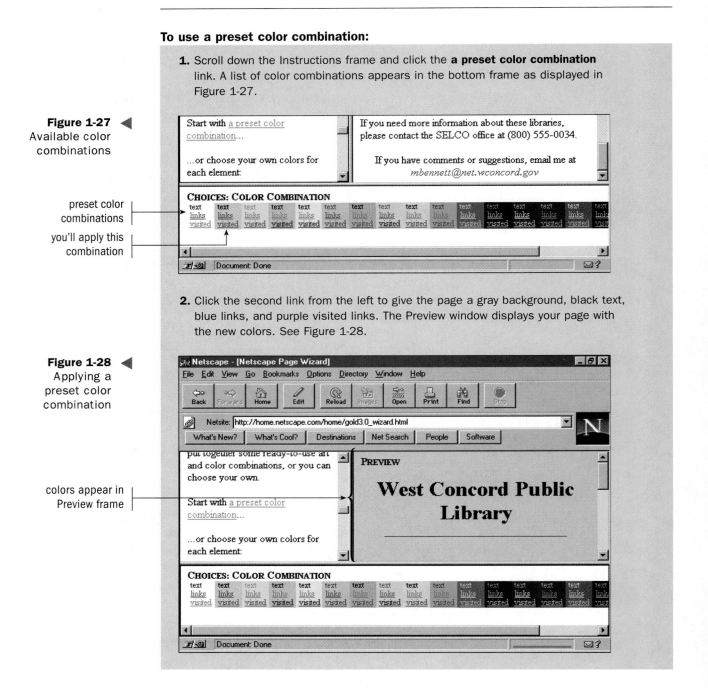

2. Click the second link from the left to give the page a gray background, black text, blue links, and purple visited links. The Preview window displays your page with the new colors. See Figure 1-28.

Figure 1-28 ◀
Applying a
preset color
combination

colors appear in
Preview frame

Changing the Color of a Single Page Element

After choosing the color scheme, you decide that you do want to change some of the colors used in the preset color combination you chose. To do this you go to the list of individual elements displayed in the Instructions frame. When you click an entry from that list, the Choices frame presents a band of color options from which you can select a color or pattern for that particular element. You decide you'd like the text of your page to appear in forest green rather than in black.

To change the color of the text in your Web page:

1. Click the **text color** link in the Instructions frame. The Choices frame shows a band of colors that you can use to modify your Web page's text color.

2. Click the **forest green** color on the far right of the color strip in the Choices frame to change the color of the text to a dark forest green. You might need to scroll to the right to see this color. The Preview frame now shows the text in forest green. See Figure 1-29.

Figure 1-29 ◀
Selecting a
different
text color

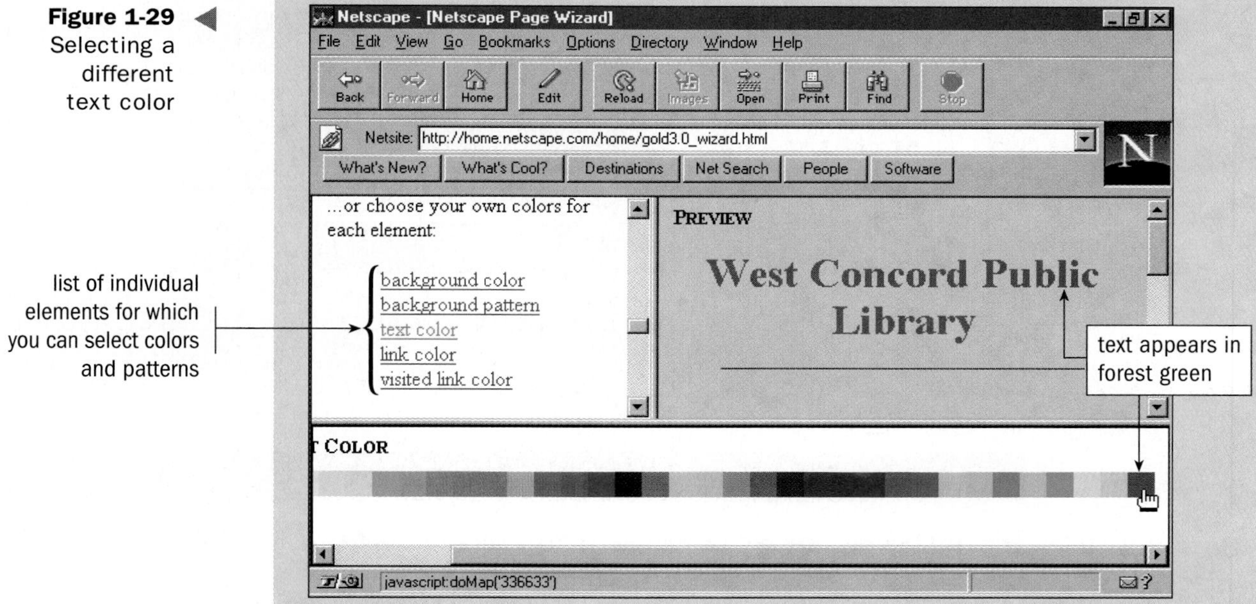

list of individual
elements for which
you can select colors
and patterns

Designing a Background

The gray background in your page seems a bit "bland" compared to other pages you've seen on the Web. The Page Wizard lets you add interest to your page with different background colors and patterns. Clicking the background color link in the Instructions frame lets you select a different background color, while clicking the background pattern link lets you select one of the Page Wizard's pre-designed background patterns. Some patterns can give your page the illusion of coming from paper with a distinct grain. Other patterns give your page a festive appearance. Whatever background you choose, make sure it does not clash with the text on your page or make your page unreadable.

To add a background pattern to your Web page:

1. Click the **background pattern** link in the Instructions frame. A list of patterns offered by the Netscape Page Wizard appears in the Choices frame. You decide to use the gray-patterned background, fearing that the other patterns, while pretty, will make your text harder to read.

2. Click the third pattern from the right. You might need to scroll to the right to see this background. The Preview frame, shown in Figure 1-30, now displays your page with a pattern of gray circles on a light gray background.

Figure 1-30
Applying a
background
pattern

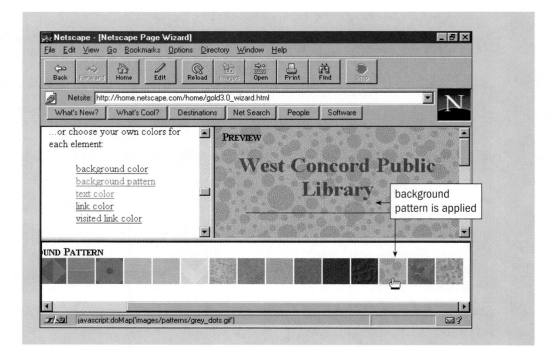

Adding Horizontal Lines and Bullets

Web pages often use bullets and horizontal lines to emphasize key points and to divide the page into readable sections. The Page Wizard has automatically added these elements to your page. Notice the horizontal lines separating the title from the introductory text, for example, and the bullets next to the links you added. You can use the default bullets and lines that the Wizard provided, or you can replace those bullet and line styles with new ones. Some of the other choices provided by the Page Wizard include lines and bullets of varying colors, some with animation. You decide to experiment with different line and bullet styles to see if they improve the appearance of your page.

To choose a different style for your bulleted list:

1. Click the **choose a bullet style** link in the Instructions frame. The Choices frame displays a selection of bullets. You decide to use the bullets with the white star on a blue background.

2. Click the **star bullet**, the fourth symbol from the left, in the bottom frame. The Preview frame changes, displaying the list of links with the new bullet style as shown in Figure 1-31.

Figure 1-31
Applying a
different bullet
style

new bullet style

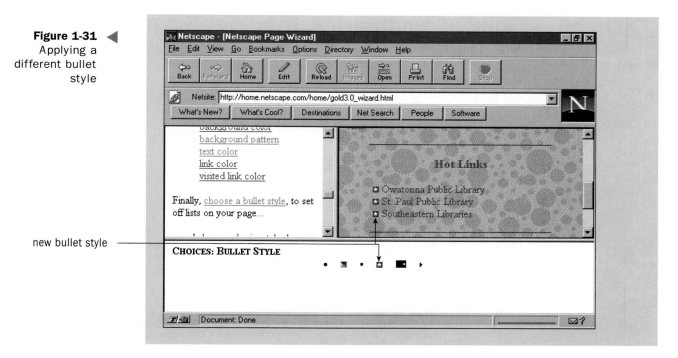

You decide now you'd like to take a look at the available line styles, and perhaps select one that adds more color to your page.

To change the horizontal line style:

1. Click the **choose a horizontal rule style** link in the Instructions frame. The bottom frame displays a selection of horizontal lines. You replace the thin black line with a thick yellow line.

2. Click the **yellow horizontal line**, the seventh from the bottom, in the Choices frame. You might have to scroll to locate this line style. The Preview frame, shown in Figure 1-32, displays the new line style in your page.

Figure 1-32
Applying a
different line
style

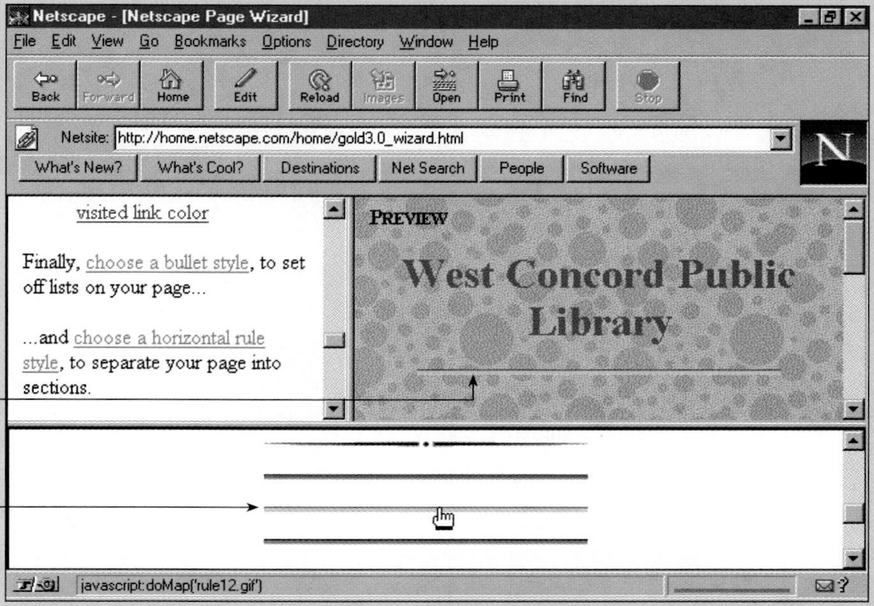

yellow line

Building and Saving Your Web Page

You've finished your first Web page. Take a few moments to look over the page in the Preview frame. If you want to make changes to any of the page elements, you can click the appropriate links in the Instructions frame. If you want to start over completely, you can click the Start Over button in the left frame. For now, though, you are satisfied with the appearance of your page. Your next step is to build and save the page. **Building** a page causes the Page Wizard to create a Web page based on your choices. This page exists on a computer supported by Netscape. Once the page is built, you can transfer the page from the Netscape computer to your computer.

Once you have built your page, you can still modify it by clicking the Back button on the Netscape toolbar to return to the Page Wizard. Netscape stores your last Page Wizard choices for as long as the Netscape browser is open.

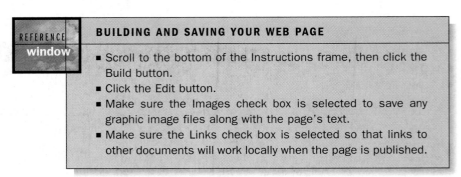

REFERENCE window

BUILDING AND SAVING YOUR WEB PAGE

- Scroll to the bottom of the Instructions frame, then click the Build button.
- Click the Edit button.
- Make sure the Images check box is selected to save any graphic image files along with the page's text.
- Make sure the Links check box is selected so that links to other documents will work locally when the page is published.

You decide to build your page and then save it on your Student Disk.

To build your Web page:

1. Scroll to the bottom of the Instructions frame to locate the Build button.

2. Click the **Build** button. Netscape builds the page and displays the complete page in the Netscape document window as shown in Figure 1-33. Building a Web page could take anywhere from a few seconds to a minute depending upon the speed of the Page Wizard and the speed of your Internet connection.

Figure 1-33 ◀
Building your
Web page

URL shows that page
currently resides at
Netscape's site

your built page

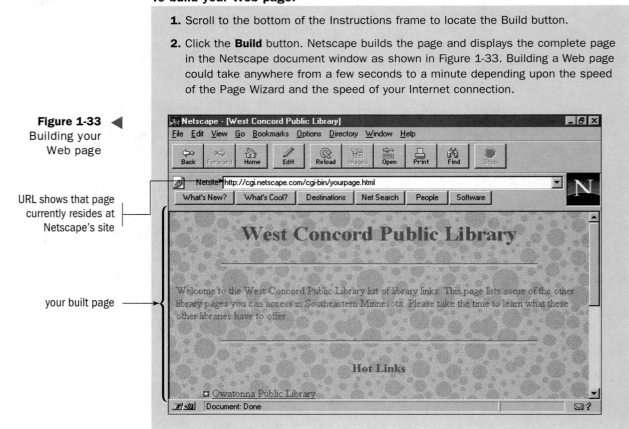

After your page has been built you will want to save it to your computer. Netscape provides a Save As command for saving the contents of Web pages. Unfortunately this command *does not* automatically save any graphic images that appear on the page. You realize that the West Concord Public Library page that you created has several graphic images—for the page background, the yellow horizontal line, and the star bullet symbol. If you used the Save As command, these features would not be saved to your computer.

To save the page, including any graphic images, you should use the Edit command on the Netscape menu or the Netscape toolbar. The Edit command will save the line style, bullet symbol, and background pattern from the page you created with the Page Wizard.

The Edit command also includes an option to adjust the URLs of links in the Web document to assist in remote publishing. This option is useful when you are transferring a collection of Web pages all located in the same folder on a remote computer and need to have the hypertext links between pages in the collection point to each other using a local address. This option doesn't apply to the West Concord Public Library page since it is a single page and not a page of a collection.

Using the Edit command also loads the page into the Netscape Editor. You can use the Netscape Editor to make further changes to the page, as you'll see in Session 1.3.

To save the West Concord Public Library page:

1. Click the **Edit** button on the Netscape toolbar. The Save Remote Document dialog box appears. See Figure 1-34.

Figure 1-34 ◄
Saving your
Web page

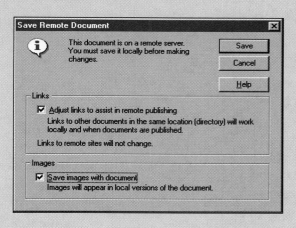

2. Verify that the **Save images with document** check box is selected.

3. Click the **Save** button.

4. Netscape might display a warning about using copyrighted materials. Since this example does not use any copyrighted materials, click the **OK** button if this dialog box appears.

5. Save the file as **Library** to the Tutorial.01 folder on your Student Disk.

   TROUBLE? If you are not sure how to set up and use your Student Disk, refer to the Read This Before You Begin discussion at the beginning of this tutorial, or talk to your instructor.

In the process of saving your Web page, five files should have been copied to your Student Disk. Figure 1-35 shows these five files.

Figure 1-35
Files saved with
your Web page

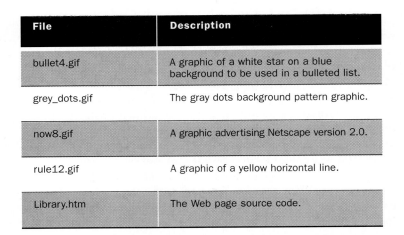

File	Description
bullet4.gif	A graphic of a white star on a blue background to be used in a bulleted list.
grey_dots.gif	The gray dots background pattern graphic.
now8.gif	A graphic advertising Netscape version 2.0.
rule12.gif	A graphic of a yellow horizontal line.
Library.htm	The Web page source code.

The **source code** is the underlying page information created by the Page Wizard. It contains information about the text on the page and the list of hypertext links. It indicates how the page should appear in terms of color, graphics, and background. The source code is the file that the browser reads when it tries to determine how to present the page to the user.

Printing Your Web Page

With the Netscape Editor now on the screen, you can print a copy of the page created by the Page Wizard to show to Muriel.

To print your Web page:

1. Click **File** then click **Print** from the Netscape Editor menu bar.

2. Choose your printer in the Print dialog box then click the **OK** button.

Now that you've saved a copy of the Web page on your Student Disk, you can further edit the document using the Netscape Editor. This can involve changing the text, modifying the page's appearance, or adding new page elements. In the next session, you'll learn how to use the Netscape Editor. For now you decide to take a break.

To exit the Netscape Editor:

1. Click **File** then click **Exit** from the Netscape menu bar.

2. Exit your Internet account.

Quick Check

1 Explain why you must be connected to the Internet to use the Netscape Page Wizard.

2 What are frames?

3 What does "building" your page with the Page Wizard do?

4 How many hypertext links can you add using the Page Wizard?

5 Name the page elements you can add with the Netscape Page Wizard.

SESSION

1.3

In this session you will learn about the Netscape Editor, a tool that comes with Netscape Navigator Gold that helps you work with Web pages. You will use the Netscape Editor to make some minor modifications to the West Concord Public Library Web page.

The Netscape Editor

Until recently, most browsers functioned only to give users access to Web documents. With the release of Netscape Navigator Gold, Netscape has added the ability to create and edit Web documents via the **Netscape Editor**. Unlike the Page Wizard, which is a Web page that allows you to create documents following a predesigned series of formats, the Netscape Editor gives you flexibility in controlling the appearance and content of your Web page. You can enter, select, and edit text on the page itself without having to work through a Choices frame such as the one in the Page Wizard. With the Netscape Editor you can:

- Retrieve a Web page off the World Wide Web, including any embedded graphics, and edit the document on your computer.
- Create a new Web document from scratch.
- Edit your documents in a near-WYSIWYG (what you see is what you get) environment, so that you will see an immediate preview of how the final document will appear.
- Quickly and easily insert graphic objects and hypertext links into your document.
- Publish your document on the Internet.

Starting the Netscape Editor

How you start the Netscape Editor depends on several things: whether you want to create a new page from scratch, whether you want to edit an existing page that is already open, or whether you want to edit a page that is not open. When you start the Netscape Editor, it opens in its own window, not the browser window.

REFERENCE
window

STARTING THE NETSCAPE EDITOR

- To create a new page from scratch, click File on the Netscape browser menu bar, point to New Document, then click Blank.
- To open an existing page that is already open in the browser, click the Edit button .
- To open an existing page that is not already open, click File, click Open File in Editor, locate and select the page you want to open, then click the Open button.

You start the Netscape browser before you access the Netscape Editor window, but unlike the Netscape browser, you can use the Netscape Editor without actually being connected to the Internet. If you are paying for your Internet connection, this can be a real money-saver. When you start the browser, your computer will probably attempt to connect to the Internet. If you are just using the Netscape Editor, click Cancel or Stop on your Internet connection dialog box to halt the connection.

One of the most powerful features of the Netscape Editor is the fact that you can retrieve any page on the Web into the Netscape Editor window. You open the page in the browser and then click the Edit button as you did in Session 1.2 with the Page Wizard page you created. This allows you to use any page on the Web as a model for your own page. Be sure, however, that if you retrieve someone else's page, you do not use any copyrighted or proprietary information.

You decide to open the Library page into the Netscape Editor window and then save it with the name Library2 so your changes don't alter the original file.

To open the Library file and save it with the name Library2:

1. Double-click the **Netscape Navigator Gold** icon ![icon] on your computer's desktop or from within the Netscape program window.

2. If your computer tries to initiate an Internet connection, click the **Cancel** button.

3. If your computer tries to load your home page off the World Wide Web, click the **Stop** button on the Netscape toolbar.

4. Click **File** then click **Open File in Editor** from the Netscape menu.

5. Locate and open the Library file from the Tutorial.01 folder on your Student Disk. The Library page appears in the Netscape Editor window.

6. Click **File** then click **Save As**.

7. Locate your Student Disk, then save the file as Library2 in the Tutorial.01 folder. See Figure 1-36.

Figure 1-36 ◀
Netscape
Editor

menu bar

toolbars

document window

status bar

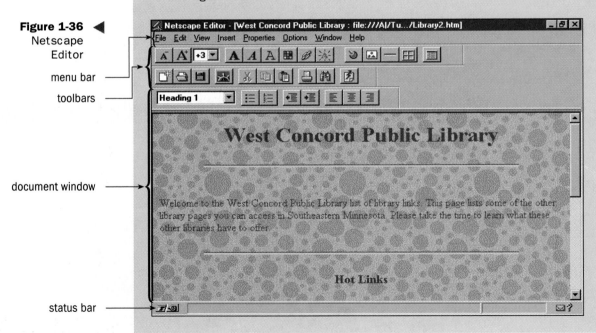

Now that your page is open in the Netscape Editor, you can add new text or modify existing text right on the page. The Netscape Editor window shown in Figure 1-36 has the features discussed in Figure 1-37.

Figure 1-37 ◀
Elements of the
Netscape Editor
window

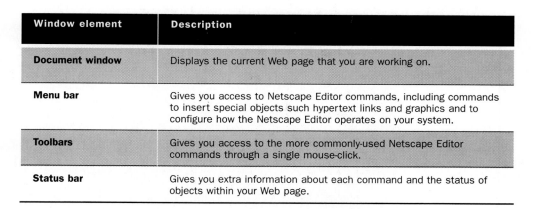

Window element	Description
Document window	Displays the current Web page that you are working on.
Menu bar	Gives you access to Netscape Editor commands, including commands to insert special objects such hypertext links and graphics and to configure how the Netscape Editor operates on your system.
Toolbars	Gives you access to the more commonly-used Netscape Editor commands through a single mouse-click.
Status bar	Gives you extra information about each command and the status of objects within your Web page.

Editing Your Web Page with the Netscape Editor

Muriel has looked over the printout of the Web page you created. She likes what you've done but wants to make a few changes to the text. Muriel sketches out how she wants the revised page to look. Muriel's revision plan is shown in Figure 1-38. You can do all the things Muriel has requested using the Netscape Editor.

Figure 1-38 ◀
Muriel's
revision plan

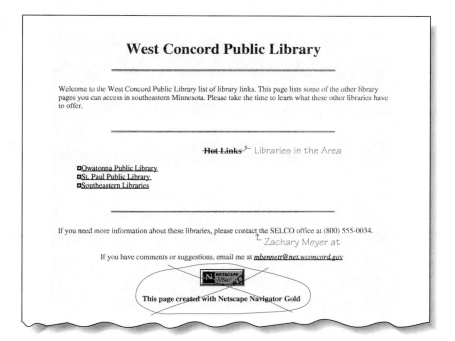

Inserting Additional Text

The first thing Muriel wants you to do is add some more information to the page. The concluding paragraph indicates that interested patrons should contact the SELCO office, but it doesn't tell them who to contact. She wants you to insert the name "Zachary Meyer" as the contact person. Inserting additional text into a Web page with the Netscape Editor works much as it would with a word processor. You move the mouse pointer to the spot on the page where you want the new text to appear, click the left mouse button, and start typing the new text.

To insert text into the Web page:

1. Scroll down until you see the concluding paragraph in the document window.

2. Move the mouse pointer between the words "**contact**" and "**the**" in the concluding paragraph and click the left mouse button.

3. Change the text to read, **please contact Zachary Meyer at the SELCO office**. The revised concluding paragraph should appear as shown in Figure 1-39.

Figure 1-39 ◀
Adding text in
the Netscape
Editor

revised conclusion

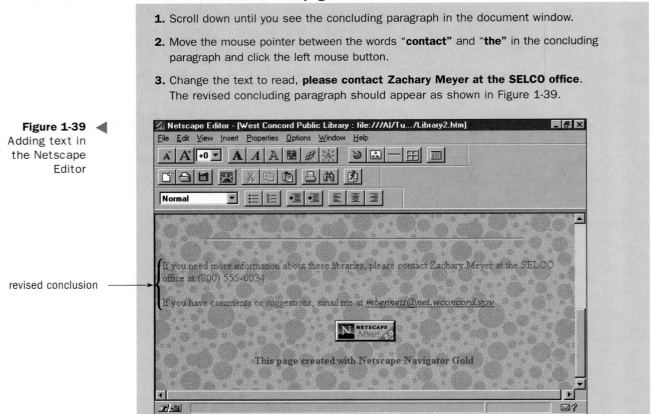

Editing Text

You check the printout in Figure 1-38 to see that Muriel next wants you to change the heading of the list of links from "Hot Links" to "Libraries in the Area." Once again you can use techniques found in most word processors to change Web page text. The most effective way to change a large block of text is to select the entire text with the mouse and to overwrite it, replacing it with new text.

To change the text of the list heading:

1. Move the mouse pointer to the beginning of the Hot Links heading.

2. Hold down the mouse button and drag the pointer over the text, **Hot Links**, selecting the entire text as shown in Figure 1-40.

Figure 1-40 ◀
Selecting text
to replace

selected text

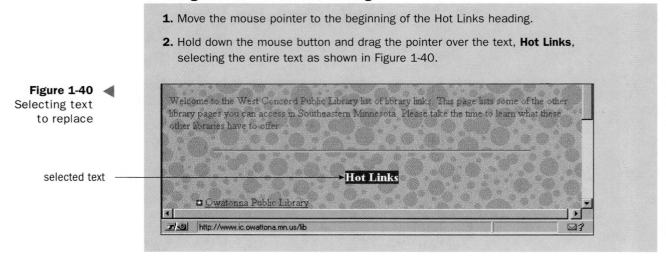

3. Type **Libraries in the Area**. Figure 1-41 shows the new heading.

Figure 1-41 ◀
New heading
for links list

new heading —

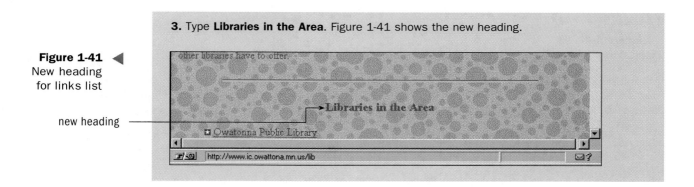

Removing Page Elements

Finally, Muriel wants you to remove the logo and text advertising for Netscape Navigator 2.0. You can remove page elements by simply selecting the objects on the page and pressing the Del key on your keyboard.

To remove the Netscape Navigator logo and text:

1. Drag the vertical scroll bar down until you see the Netscape Navigator logo and accompanying text.

2. Click the Netscape Navigator logo.

3. Press the **Del** key.

4. Highlight the text, **This page created with Netscape Navigator Gold**, and press the **Del** key.

TROUBLE? Some versions of the Netscape Editor move one or more of the horizontal lines to the left. To correct this problem, click the horizontal line, then click the Center button .

To save and then print a copy of the revised Web page:

1. Click **File**, then click **Save**.

2. Click **File** then click **Print**.

3. Select the printer you want to use.

4. Click the **OK** button. The final printout looks like Figure 1-42.

TROUBLE? If your printout includes header and footer information, don't worry. Your Netscape print options are set differently.

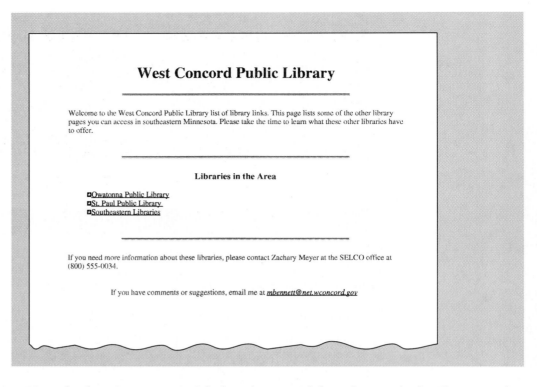

You take the printout to Muriel; she is happy with how the page looks. She is sure that over the course of your internship the two of you will be able to work on the page and improve it and add to it. For now you can quit the Netscape Editor.

To quit the Netscape Editor:

1. Click **File** then click **Exit**.

2. If necessary, click **Yes** to exit Netscape.

Getting Online Help for Netscape

If you have any future questions about using the Netscape browser or editor, Muriel suggests you look at Netscape's online help. Netscape's help information is stored in a handbook available on the World Wide Web. The page itself is being constantly changed and revised as new versions of the browser and editor appear.

To access the Netscape handbook:

1. If necessary, connect to your Internet account on your campus network or with your Internet Service Provider and then start Netscape.

2. Click **Help** then click **Handbook** from the Netscape menu in either the browser or editor window.

3. The handbook appears in the document window as shown in Figure 1-43.

   TROUBLE? If your page does not match the one shown in Figure 1-43, Netscape might have updated the Handbook.

Figure 1-43 ◀
Getting help
from the
Handbook

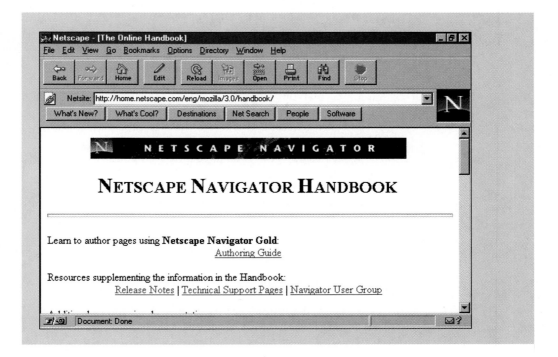

Information about using the Netscape Editor is contained on another Web page called the Authoring Guide. A link to this page is placed on the Netscape Handbook page.

To access the Authoring Guide:

1. Click the **Authoring Guide** link. The Netscape browser displays the contents of the Authoring Guide. You can get help from the Authoring Guide page by following the links that look most applicable.

2. Click **File**, then click **Exit** to exit Netscape.

3. Exit your Internet account.

Quick Check

1. Do you have to be connected to the Internet to use the Netscape Editor?

2. How do you replace text?

3. Describe how you would open the page located at http://www.whitehouse.gov for editing.

4. Where can you find Help on using the Netscape browser?

Tutorial Assignments

Muriel Bennett at West Concord Public Library has another page she wants you to design. She wants a page titled "Twin Cities Libraries" that displays links to libraries in the Minneapolis/St. Paul area. The links are:

Metronet	http://www.metronet.lib.mn.us/
State Government Libraries	http://www.state.mn.us/libraries/calco.html
Twin Cities Catalog	http://www.stpaul.lib.mn.us/pages/metrolibraries.html
St. Paul Library	http://www.stpaul.lib.mn.us/

The list of links should have the title "Web Pages." She wants the text of the page to be black on a yellow-green background. Linked text should be shown in red. She does not want any background pattern. Muriel would like you to use triangles as bullets in the list of library links. She wants different sections of the page separated by a red line.

To create a page matching Muriel's description:

1. Access your Internet account with either your Internet Service Provider or Campus Network.
2. Start Netscape and access the Netscape Page Wizard.
3. Start the Page Wizard.
4. Click the "give your page a title" link and type "Twin Cities Libraries" in the Title box.
5. Click the "type an introduction" link and type "These are some library resources in the Twin Cities area." in the Introduction box.
6. Click the "add some hot links" link and enter the links to the Web pages that Muriel has given you.
7. Click the "type a paragraph of text" link and type "Click the highlighted text to access the Web page." in the Conclusion box.
8. Click the "add an e-mail link" link and type your own e-mail address in the E-mail link text box.
9. Click the "preset color combination" link and choose the fourth link from the left (black text on a yellow-green background).
10. Click the "choose a bullet style" link and choose the triangle bullet style (the last bullet on the right).
11. Click the "choose a horizontal rule style" link and choose the red horizontal line (the sixth choice from the bottom).
12. Click the Build button.
13. Click the Edit button on the Netscape toolbar.
14. Save your Web page as Library3 to the Tassign folder in the Tutorial.01 folder on your Student Disk.
15. Change the title of the list of library links to "Web Pages."
16. Save your changes to the page.
17. Print a copy of the page.
18. Exit the Netscape browser and Netscape Editor and your Internet account.
19. Hand in your printout to your instructor.

Case Problems

1. Creating a Page for the MidWest University Theater Department You are a graduate assistant in the Theater Department at MidWest University. The head of the department, Dennis Paige, wants your help in designing a Web page entitled "Shakespeare on the Web" for students on the works of William Shakespeare. The page will contain links to sites that store copies and commentaries on Shakespeare's plays and his life and times. Professor Paige has four links that he wants you to place on the page, following the heading "Links to Shakespeare Resources":

The Works of Shakespeare
    http://the-tech.mit.edu/Shakespeare/works.html
Shakespeare's Sonnets
    http://quarles.unbc.edu/shakescan/
The Royal Shakespeare Company
    http://www.hiway.co.uk/ei/rsc.html
Shakespeare Illustrated
    http://www.cc.emory.edu/ENGLISH/classes/Shakespeare_Illustrated/Shakespeare.html

Include a brief description of the page and directions on how to use the page in the concluding paragraph. He leaves the page design up to you. Since you will be maintaining the page, he wants you to place a link to your e-mail address in the page.

To create this page:
1. Access your Internet account.
2. In the Editor, start Netscape and access the Netscape Page Wizard.
3. Start the Page Wizard.
4. Click the "give your page a title" link and type "Shakespeare on the Web" in the Title box.
5. Click the "type an introduction" link and type a description of the page's purpose.
6. Click the "add some hot links" link and enter the links to the Web pages that Professor Paige has given you.
7. Click the "type a paragraph of text" link and enter directions on how to use the page for new users.
8. Click the "add an e-mail link" link and type your own e-mail address in the E-mail link box.
9. Choose a color combination, background style, bullet style, and horizontal line style for your page.
10. Click the Build button.
11. Click the Edit button on the Netscape toolbar.
12. Save your Web page as Bard to the Cases folder in the Tutorial.01 folder on your Student Disk.
13. Change the title of the list of library links to "Links to Shakespeare Resources."
14. Save your changes to the page.
15 Print a copy of the page.
16. Exit the Netscape browser and Netscape Editor and your Internet account.
17. Hand in the printout to your instructor.

2. Creating a Page for the King Middle School You are a new teacher of 6th and 7th graders at King Middle School. The school has recently obtained a connection to the Web. You're anxious to create a Web page for your students that connects them to pages designed for kids. A colleague of yours at another school has already created such a page. She has shared the file that contains her page for you to copy and modify for your own needs.

To complete this assignment:
1. Open the Netscape Editor. You do not have to be connected to the Internet.
2. Open the file School.htm in the Cases folder in the Tutorial.01 folder of your Student Disk.
3. Change the title of the page to "King Middle School."
4. Overwrite the introductory paragraph, inserting the text: "To meet other kids your age on the Web, click one of the titles in the list below."
5. Replace the heading for a list of pages with "Web Pages for Kids."
6. Insert your name in the concluding paragraph.
7. Save the page as School2 in the Cases folder of the Tutorial.01 folder on your Student Disk.
8. Print a copy of the page.
9. Hand in your printout to your instructor.

3. Creating a Web Page Resume You are about to graduate and you want to create a resume page that you can later post on the World Wide Web. A friend tells you that you can get a resume document off the Web, which you can edit to include information about yourself. The URL for the resume page is:
http://www2.coursetools.com/cti/NewPerspectives/web/resume.html/
1. Access your Internet account.
2. Start the Netscape browser.
3. Click the Open button on the Netscape toolbar and type the URL in the Open Location text box.
4. After the page is finished loading, click the Edit button on the Netscape toolbar.
5. Save the page and accompanying graphics to your student disk under the name **resume** in the Tutorial.01 folder on your Student Disk.

6. Edit the page, placing your name in the title and your job history in the main text.
7. Save the page as **Resume2** in the Cases folder in the Tutorial.01 folder on your Student Disk.
8. Print a copy of your page.
9. Hand in the printout to your instructor.

4. Creating your own home page Using the Netscape Page Wizard, create your own home page. Include four links to your favorite Web pages. In the introductory paragraph include some information about yourself. Insert your favorite quote in the closing paragraph. Choose whatever color combination or design elements you think will make your page interesting and attractive. Include a link to your e-mail address. Save the page to the Cases folder in the Tutorial.01 folder of your Student disk with the name "Homepage," then print the page for your instructor.

Lab Assignments

LAB

The Internet
World Wide Web

This Lab Assignment is designed to accompany the interactive Course Lab called Internet World Wide Web. **To start the Lab using Windows 95,** click the Start button on the Windows 95 taskbar, point to Programs, point to Course Labs, point to New Perspectives Applications, and click Internet World Wide Web. **To start the Lab using Windows 3.1,** double-click the Course Labs for the Internet group icon to open a window containing the Lab icons, then double-click the Internet World Wide Web icon. If you do not see Course Labs on your Windows 95 Programs menu, or if you do not see the Course Labs for the Internet group icon in your Windows 3.1 Program Manager window, see your instructor or technical support person.

1. The Internet: World Wide Web One of the most popular services on the Internet is the World Wide Web. This Lab is a Web simulator that teaches you how to use Web browser software to find information. You can use this Lab whether or not your school provides you with Internet access.

1. Click the Steps button to learn how to use Web browser software. As you proceed through the Steps, answer all the Quick Check questions that appear. After you complete the Steps, you will see a Quick Check Summary Report. Follow the instructions on the screen to print this report.
2. Click the Explore button on the Welcome screen. Use the Web browser to locate a weather map of the Caribbean Virgin Islands. What is its URL?
3. Enter the URL **http://www.atour.com**. A SCUBA diver named Wadson Lachouffe has been searching for the fabled treasure of Greybeard the pirate. A link from the Adventure Travel Web site leads to Wadson's Web page called "Hidden Treasure." Locate the Hidden Treasure page, and answer the following questions:
   What was the name of Greybeard's ship?
   What was Greybeard's favorite food?
   What does Wadson think happened to Greybeard's ship?
4. In the Steps, you found a graphic of Jupiter from the photo archives of the Jet Propulsion Laboratory. In the Explore section of the Lab, you can also find a graphic of Saturn. Suppose one of your friends wants a picture of Saturn for an astronomy report. Make a list of the blue, underlined links your friend must click to find the Saturn graphic. Assume that your friend begins at the Web Trainer home page.
5. Jump back to the Adventure Travel Web site. Write a one-page description of the information at the site, including the number of pages the site contains, and diagram the links it contains.
6. Chris Thomson, a student at UVI, has his own Web page. In Explore, look at the information Chris included on his page. Suppose you could create your own Web page. What would you include? Use word-processing software to design your own Web page. Make sure to indicate the graphics and links you would use.

Working with the Netscape Editor

Creating a Home Page

OBJECTIVES

In this tutorial you will:

- View and open a Netscape template

- Create a Web page from scratch in the Netscape Editor

- Define a Web page's properties

- Format large sections of text using paragraph tags

- Format individual characters or words using character tags

- Insert and format graphic images

- Create a Web page background

CASE

Creating the Avalon Books Home Page

You work at Avalon Books, a large bookstore in the city of Lakeside. The store offers its customers more than books; it also includes reading rooms, play areas for the kids, and a small café. The bookstore sponsors special events such as author signings, poetry readings, and live music. The manager of Avalon Books, Mark Stewart, has asked you to create a Web page to advertise Avalon Books on the World Wide Web.

Netscape provides three methods to create a Web page. You've already worked with the Page Wizard method, in which you select page elements from a list to build your page. Your opportunity for creativity when using the Page Wizard is limited to this preselected list. A second method of creating a new page is using a **template**, a professionally designed page that you retrieve and use as a model for your own page. Although using a template relieves you from having to spend time on page design, you might find that the template designs don't appeal to you or that your page ends up looking like a lot of other pages whose creators have also used the templates. You can use both the Page Wizard and the templates to "jump start" your page by creating the page and then using the Netscape Editor to modify it. A third method of creating a new page is starting from scratch with a blank page in the Netscape Editor. You enter and format your own text and create your own design using the Netscape Editor tools.

You decide to start your work with the Avalon Books Web page by examining the Netscape templates to see whether they might fit the scheme Mark has in mind.

In this session you will learn how to access predesigned Web page templates using the Netscape browser. Then you'll use the Netscape Editor to begin creating a Web page from scratch. You will learn how to define properties for your document and to enter and then format text in your page.

Viewing Netscape Templates

To help new users construct Web pages, Netscape has created several sample Web pages for users to retrieve and edit. These pages cover topics ranging from creating a home page of your personal interests to designing a page for a small business. Each template contains sample text, graphics, and links. Once you've retrieved a template, you replace the sample text with your own text and alter the graphics and links as necessary. You can then save the altered template on your own computer and publish it as your own page.

You can actually retrieve any page on the Web with Netscape and edit it—not just the Netscape templates—so any Web page can function as a template. However, you should keep in mind that most Web pages contain copyrighted material that you cannot use without permission. The Netscape templates, however, have no such restrictions. You are free to open and adapt them however you want.

REFERENCE
window

ACCESSING A NETSCAPE TEMPLATE

- Connect to the Internet.
- Open the Netscape browser.
- Choose File, point to New Document, then click From Template.
- Click the hypertext link for the template you want to use.
- Click the Edit button [⬛] to retrieve the template html file and accompanying graphics files.
- Edit the template as necessary in the Netscape Editor and save it on your computer when you are finished.

As a first step in creating the Avalon page, you decide to take a look at what the Netscape templates have to offer. Even if you decide against using the template, it could give you some ideas about creating your own page.

To view the Netscape Web Page Templates page:

1. Start the Netscape browser and access your Internet account.

   TROUBLE?　If you don't know how to access your Internet account, talk to your instructor or a technical support person in the computer lab in which you are working.

2. Click **File**, point to **New Document**, then click **From Template**. The browser opens the Netscape Web Page Templates page.

3. Scroll down to view the list of templates shown in Figure 2-1.

   TROUBLE?　Your browser window might show more or less of the templates page, depending on your monitor's resolution. Maximize the Netscape window to see more of the page.

Figure 2-1 ◀
Template
categories

first three categories
of templates

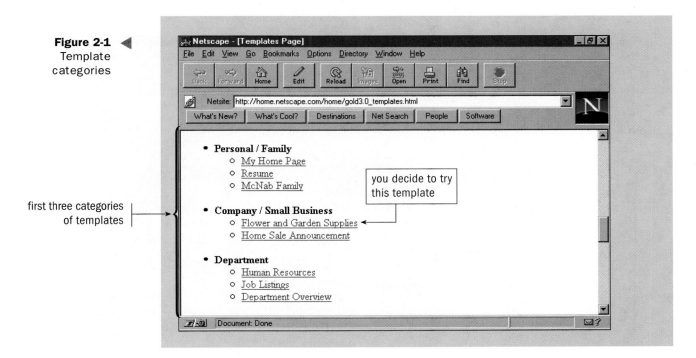

Netscape has grouped its available templates into six categories, the first three of which are shown in Figure 2-1.

- Personal/Family

- Company/Small Business

- Department

- Product/Service

- Special Interest Group

- Interesting and Fun

Because Avalon Books is a small business, you decide the second category, Company / Small Business, is the most appropriate.

To open a Netscape template:

1. Scroll the document window until you can see the Company/Small Business category.

2. Click the **Flower and Garden Supplies** hypertext link. Scroll down to see the template, shown in Figure 2-2.

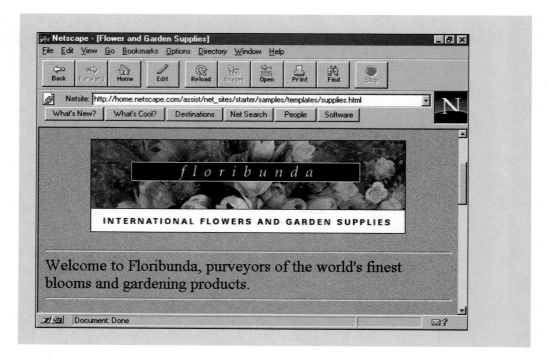

At this point, if you wanted to use the template you could click the Edit button on the toolbar. Clicking the Edit button retrieves all the text and graphics associated with the Web page. You would then edit the page to meet your needs. You would not have to spend any time on page design as the template provides a design for you. Templates thus can be a great starting point for new Web page authors who don't want to spend a lot of time on page design.

Before retrieving this template, you decide to ask Mark for his opinion on its applicability. Mark examines the template and then shows you the flyer shown in Figure 2-3. He explains that he uses this flyer to advertise the bookstore's current events.

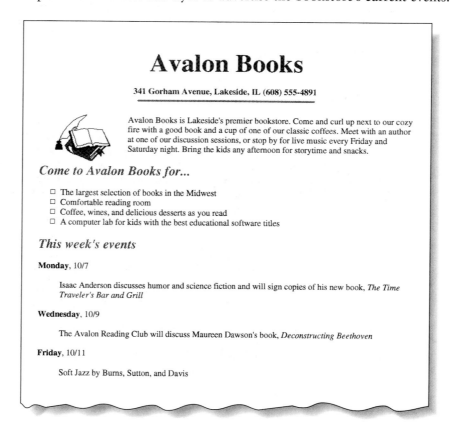

Mark wants the Avalon Books Web page to duplicate the appearance of the flyer in Figure 2-3 as closely as possible. You both agree that, as nice as the Floribunda template is, it would take more work to change it to fit the flyer's design than to simply create the page from scratch. You therefore decide to use the Netscape Editor to create an entirely new page.

Creating a New Document in the Netscape Editor

Recall that you access the Netscape Editor from the Netscape browser. When the page you want to edit is already open in the browser, you can click the Edit button to place the current page into the editor. However, when you want to edit a page other than the one that currently appears in the browser, or you want to create a page from scratch, you use the File menu options, not the Edit button.

To create a new document in the Netscape Editor:

1. Since you no longer need to use the resources of the Internet, disconnect from your Internet account but do not close the Netscape browser.

2. In the Netscape browser, click **File**, point at **New Document**, then click **Blank**. The Netscape Editor opens to a blank page. See Figure 2-4.

   TROUBLE? If your toolbars are in a different order or location than those shown in Figure 2-4, don't worry. If no toolbars appear, click Options on the menu bar, then click the toolbar names, one at a time, to make them appear.

Figure 2-4 ◀
A blank document in the Netscape Editor

File/Edit toolbar

Paragraph Format toolbar

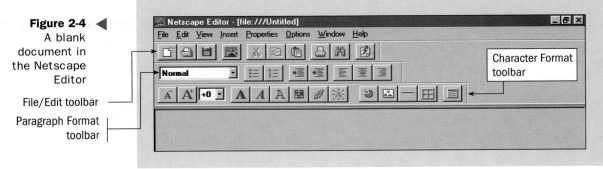

In the previous tutorial you used the Netscape Editor to edit and replace text. Now you'll use it to create page elements from scratch. The most efficient way of creating new page elements is through the Netscape Editor toolbars, described in Figure 2-5.

Figure 2-5 ◀
Netscape Editor toolbars

Toolbar	Description
File/Edit	Contains options for file management tasks such as saving a Web page, opening a saved file, printing a page, and publishing a page on a Web server.
Paragraph Format	Contains options for modifying the appearance of paragraphs, including creating bulleted or numbered lists, indenting a paragraph, or specifying whether the paragraph should be left-, centered-, or right-aligned.
Character Format	Contains options for formatting text and other objects, including bolding and italicizing text and specifying font color. Also contains options for inserting graphic images and hypertext links.

To learn the function of each toolbar button, you can move the mouse pointer ⬚ over the button. After a second, a description of the button appears.

Setting Document Properties

Before you actually begin entering text into your new document, you should fill out the Document Properties dialog box, which stores information about your page, including a title, a description, the author, and other record-keeping details. None of the information you enter in the Document Properties dialog box appears on the page itself. Instead, Netscape uses this information to identify your page to other users, as well as to provide background information on the page. Although you don't have to fill out this dialog box, it does allow you to include additional information about you and your page—information that might not be appropriate to include on the page itself.

The Document Properties dialog box also allows you to specify **keywords**—descriptive words that identify the contents of your page to other Internet users—and classification labels that classify your page. For the Avalon Books Web page, you might enter the keywords "books" or "bookstore." Internet search pages such as the popular one developed by Yahoo use keywords to categorize a page in their Web page database. An Internet user who searches for information on books is more likely to locate the bookstore's page if you've included keywords. Since Mark has told you that he wants a lot of people to find this page, you decide to include keywords when you enter the document's properties.

To enter information for your Web page:

1. Click **Properties**, then click **Document**.

2. If necessary, click the **General** sheet tab.

3. Click the **Title** box, type **Avalon Books**, then press **Tab**.

4. Type your name in the Author box, then press **Tab**.

5. Type **This is the home page for the Avalon Books bookstore** in the Description box, then press **Tab**.

6. Type **Avalon, books, bookstores, novels, Lakeside** in the Keywords box, then press **Tab**.

   TROUBLE? Don't worry about typing keywords in upper or lowercase. Search tools don't care.

7. Type **bookstore** in the Classification box. Figure 2-6 shows the completed dialog box.

Figure 2-6 ◀
Properties of the Avalon Books Web page

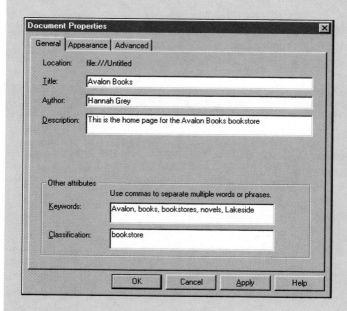

8. Click the **OK** button.

Note that the Netscape Editor's title bar now displays the title you specified. This title will also appear in the browser's title bar when other people access your page.

Before adding any text to your page, you should save the blank page to your Student Disk.

To save the Avalon Books page:

1. Click **File**, then click **Save As**.

2. Locate then select the drive containing your Student Disk.

3. Open the **Tutorial.02** folder.

4. Type **Avalon** in the File name box.

5. Click the **Save** button to save your new Web page document in the Tutorial.02 folder on your Student Disk.

Markup Tags

The Netscape Editor works much like a word processor. However, there are some important differences between a document created with a software program such as Microsoft Word and one created by the Netscape Editor for use on the Web. When you create a document using the Netscape Editor, you are actually creating a file that consists of HTML codes. **HTML**, which stands for Hypertext Markup Language, is a language in which a Web page is written. HTML uses special codes to describe how the page should appear on the screen. Figure 2-7 shows a Web page as it appears on your computer screen, and behind it, the underlying HTML code. It is this code that is actually transferred over the Web when someone accesses your page.

Figure 2-7 ◀
New Web page
and the HTML
code it employs

Web page as it
appears in the
browser and editor

An example of a
markup tag

Underlying HTML
code

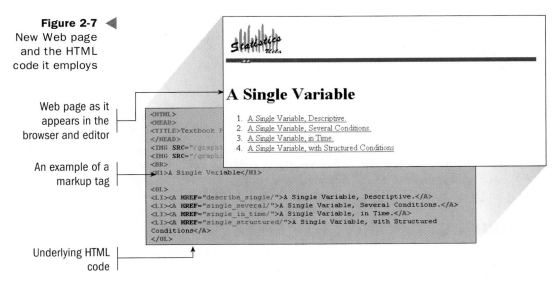

When the HTML code is transferred over the Web, the browser accessing the page interprets the code to determine the page's appearance. The appearance of each element in the page, such as a heading or a bulleted list, is indicated by a **markup tag**—a label within angle brackets that identifies the element to a browser. A tag with the label <H1>, for example, stands for "Heading 1" and indicates that the text that follows is a top-level heading in the document. Markup tags are necessarily very general so that many different kinds of browsers can read the document and determine how to display it. Not all browsers display text the same way. Some browsers, called **text-based browsers**, often can't display formatting such as bold or italics and might be able to display only one type of font. These browsers will display Heading 1 text very differently from a browser like Netscape that can display a variety of fonts and formatting. Figure 2-8 shows how two different browsers might interpret text formatted with a Heading 1 tag.

Figure 2-8 ◀
The same
heading as it
appears in
different
browsers

This is Heading 1
This is Heading 1

You might wonder why you can't simply specify that Heading 1 should be formatted in a 14 point bolded Times Roman font. However, a text-based browser would not be able to display your heading. By using a tag, you simply indicate that the text should be formatted as "Heading 1" and allow each Web browser to determine what that means.

As a Web page author, you don't have the same kind of control over your page's appearance as you would in creating a word-processed document. You can't alter the definition of a particular tag, because in the end, the appearance of text formatted with that tag is determined by the browser, not by you. You also can't create new tags. Web documents need to work with a common set of tags and would not recognize any new tags or styles that you create.

Even with these limitations, you can still create interesting and visually attractive documents. And as the Web increases in popularity, new tags will be developed that give Web authors more flexibility and control in creating pages.

In creating your Avalon Books Web page, you'll be using tags with the following document elements:

- paragraphs
- individual characters
- graphic images
- hypertext links
- tables

Not all tags are necessarily displayed in the browser. Some tags simply contain information about the document. When you were entering document information earlier you were actually inserting tags of this kind into your document. While these tags do not show up on the page, they do appear in the HTML code.

Applying Heading Styles

You are now ready to start formatting the Avalon Books Web page to mirror the appearance of Mark's flyer. As you look over Mark's flyer from Figure 2-3, you identify the following elements:

- main heading for the title
- smaller heading listing store's address and phone number
- heading for each of the two sections of the document
- bulleted list of activities at the bookstore
- bolded and italicized weekdays on which Avalon Books has scheduled events
- indented descriptions of events
- horizontal line separating headings
- graphic that makes the page visually attractive

In trying to recreate this flyer on the Web, you will need to apply a tag to each of these elements: headings, bulleted lists, formatted text, indented text, and graphics. The Netscape Editor makes it easy for you to choose the appropriate tags for each element. When you want to apply the style to an entire paragraph you choose a **paragraph tag**. When you want to apply a style to just a phrase, word, or character, you choose a **character tag**.

To start, you decide to apply the paragraph tags for the headings. HTML offers six different heading tags, labeled H1, H2, H3, and so on through H6. Netscape makes it easy to apply an HTML tag to a paragraph. Netscape has assigned a style name to each HTML tag and placed all available style names on a list that is available through the Paragraph Format toolbar. The HTML tag H1, for example, appears as the Heading 1 style in this list. Figure 2-9 shows how a typical browser might display paragraphs with each of these heading tags applied.

Figure 2-9 ◀
Heading styles
as they appear
in browser

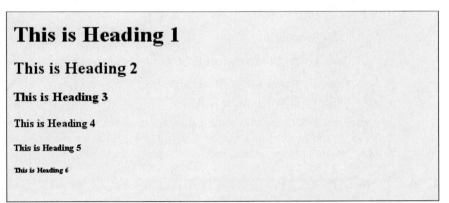

To apply a style to a paragraph, you click anywhere in the paragraph and then choose the style you want from the Paragraph style list. You can apply a style before or after you type the paragraph, and you can apply a different style at any time.

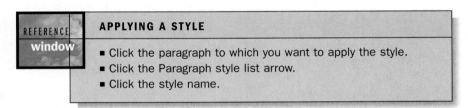

REFERENCE
window

APPLYING A STYLE

- Click the paragraph to which you want to apply the style.
- Click the Paragraph style list arrow.
- Click the style name.

You decide to use the Heading 1 style (corresponding to the H1 HTML tag) for the page's main heading, "Avalon Books," and the Heading 4 style (corresponding to the H4 HTML tag) for the store's address and phone number.

To apply the appropriate heading styles to the first two paragraphs:

1. Click the upper-left corner of the document window. The blinking insertion point indicates you are ready to type.

2. Click the **Paragraph style** list arrow ▾ on the Paragraph Format toolbar. The list of available styles opens. Each style corresponds to an HTML tag. See Figure 2-10.

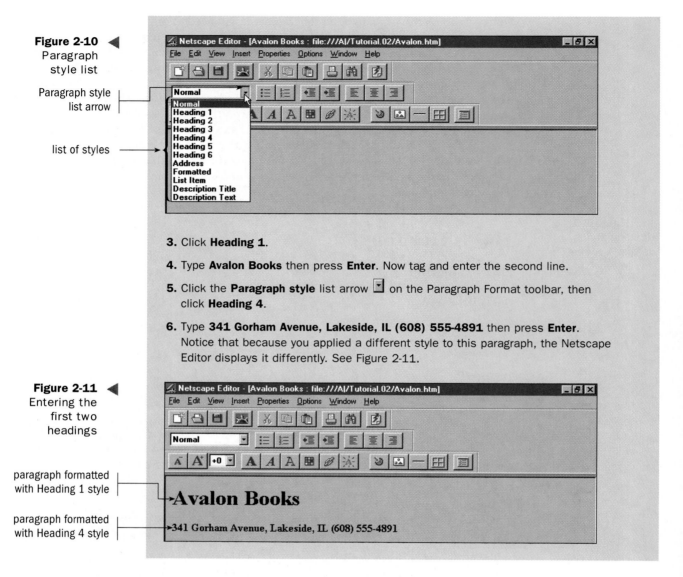

Figure 2-10
Paragraph
style list

Paragraph style
list arrow

list of styles

3. Click **Heading 1**.

4. Type **Avalon Books** then press **Enter**. Now tag and enter the second line.

5. Click the **Paragraph style** list arrow ⊡ on the Paragraph Format toolbar, then click **Heading 4**.

6. Type **341 Gorham Avenue, Lakeside, IL (608) 555-4891** then press **Enter**. Notice that because you applied a different style to this paragraph, the Netscape Editor displays it differently. See Figure 2-11.

Figure 2-11
Entering the
first two
headings

paragraph formatted
with Heading 1 style

paragraph formatted
with Heading 4 style

Within each tag, you can make some additional choices regarding the appearance of text formatted with that tag. These choices are called **properties**. While tag properties are not as extensive as what you may be accustomed to with word processors, you can still use them to add variety and interest to your text. One such property for a paragraph tag is alignment. Paragraphs can be left-, centered, or right-aligned.

You decide to center the two headings you just created to follow the format of the flyer.

To center the headings on the page:

1. Use the mouse to select the two headings.

   TROUBLE? To select the two headings, drag the mouse with the left mouse button held down from the left side of the first heading to the right side of the second.

2. Click the **Center** button ≣. Your headings are centered as in Figure 2-12.

Figure 2-12
Centered
headings

center button

selected headings are
now centered

You now add the next two headings to the page. Unlike the first two, they will be aligned with the left edge of the page.

To add additional headings:

1. Click the end of the second line and press **Enter**.

2. Click the **Align Left** button on the Paragraph Format toolbar.

3. Type **Come to Avalon Books for...** then press **Enter**.

4. Type **This week's events**, then press **Enter**.

5. Select the two headings you just entered, then click **Heading 2** from the Paragraph style list. See Figure 2-13.

Figure 2-13
Entering the
next two
headings

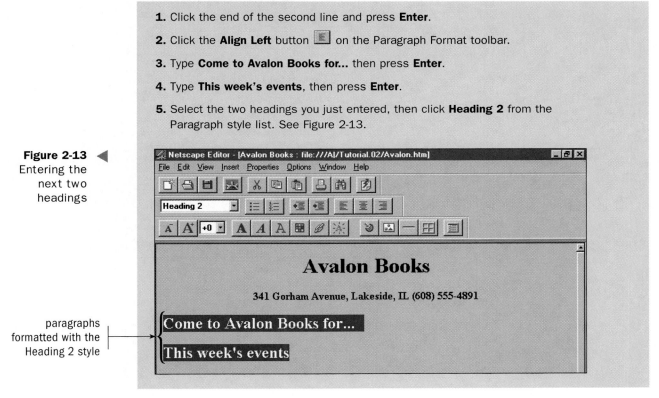

paragraphs
formatted with the
Heading 2 style

Applying the Normal Text Style

Unformatted sections of text such as descriptive or informational paragraphs are called **normal text**. You tag normal text with the Normal style. Mark's flyer includes a paragraph describing Avalon Books attractions. You are ready to enter this information into your Web page.

To add normal text to a page:

1. Click the end of the line containing Avalon Book's address and press **Enter**. When you press Enter, Netscape automatically formats the next paragraph with the Normal style, as you can see from the Paragraph style list box.

2. Click the **Align Left** button on the Paragraph Format toolbar.

3. Type the following text into the document window:

   Avalon Books is Lakeside's premier bookstore. Come and curl up next to our cozy fire with a good book and a cup of one of our classic coffees. Meet with an author at one of our discussion sessions, or stop by for live music every Friday and Saturday night. Bring the kids any afternoon for storytime and snacks.

   Your page should now look like Figure 2-14.

Figure 2-14 ◀
Entering
normal text

normal text ────▶

You are satisfied with your page so far. You decide to save your work and then take a break.

To save your changes to the Avalon Books Web page:

1. Click the **Save** button.

2. Click **File**, then click **Exit**. Netscape asks whether you want to close all windows and exit Netscape. Choosing "Yes" will close the Netscape Editor and any Netscape browser windows you have open.

3. Click the **Yes** button.

Quick Check

1. What are the Netscape templates, and how do you access them?

2. Why should you enter keywords for your Web page?

3. What are the three Netscape Editor toolbars, and what are they used for?

4 What is a markup tag?

5 What is a paragraph tag? What is a character tag?

6 How does the Netscape Editor differ from a word processor like Microsoft Word?

7 Why does the Netscape Editor prohibit you from creating your own tags?

SESSION

2.2

In this session you will learn how to enhance the appearance of your documents with ordered and unordered lists and how to format text using character formats.

Creating Lists

You can use the Netscape Editor to create two kinds of lists: a numbered list or a bulleted list. A numbered list is known as an **ordered list** because it has an order to it. You use an ordered list when you want to display, for example, an ordered outline or a list of the steps needed to complete a task. You can also create a bulleted list, known as an **unordered list**, because the order doesn't matter, and you usually distinguish between items in the list with bullet symbols. You decide to try both the ordered list and the unordered list format so you can decide how you want the list of Avalon attractions on Mark's flyer to look. First, you must reopen the page you were working on in Session 2.1.

REFERENCE window

CREATING AN ORDERED LIST

- Click the Numbered List button 📋.
- Type each list item, pressing the Enter key after each line.
- Click the Numbered List button 📋 again.

To reopen the Avalon page in the Netscape Editor:

1. Restart Netscape Navigator. You do not have to initiate an Internet connection nor load your home page.

2. Click **File**, then click **Open File in Editor**.

3. In the Open dialog box, locate the drive containing your Student Disk, open the **Tutorial.02** folder, click **Avalon.htm**, then click the **Open** button. Your Avalon Books page opens in the Netscape Editor window.

Creating an Ordered List

You decide to enter the list of Avalon attractions first as an ordered list using the Numbered List style. This style has its own toolbar button that you use instead of the Paragraph style list.

To create an ordered list:

1. Click the end of the **Come to Avalon Books for...** heading then press **Enter**.

2. Click the **Numbered List** button 📋 on the Paragraph Format toolbar. The # symbol appears—you'll see what this means in a moment.

3. Type **The largest selection of books in the Midwest**, then press **Enter**.

4. Continue entering the following items in the list, each on its own line:

   Comfortable reading rooms

   Coffee, wines, and delicious desserts as you read

   A computer lab for kids with the best educational software titles

   The Avalon Books page should now appear as shown in Figure 2-15.

   TROUBLE? If you pressed Enter after the last item in the list, press the Backspace key to remove the extra blank line.

Figure 2-15 ◄
Entering an
ordered list

ordered list ⎯⎯⎯⎯

symbol indicates
numbers will appear
in browser

Viewing Your List in the Browser

Up until now, the Netscape Editor has shown your page just as it will appear to anyone accessing it from the Netscape browser. However, this is not always the case. For example, when you create an ordered list, the Netscape Editor does not display the numbers in the ordered list. Instead the numbers are represented by a double pound sign (##). To see how these numbers will appear to someone accessing the page in a browser, you must actually view the page in the browser window. You can switch from the Netscape Editor window to the browser window to view how the browser automatically replaces the ## with numbers.

To view the numbered list in the Netscape browser window:

1. Click the **Save** button 💾 to save your changes to the page.

2. Click the **View in Browser** button 🖥 on the File/Edit toolbar. The page appears in the browser as shown in Figure 2-16. The ordered list now appears with numbers. This is how your page will look to other Netscape users. Different browsers might display it differently.

Figure 2-16 ◀
Viewing the
page in the
browser

symbol appears as
numbers in browser

Creating an Unordered List

An unordered list uses bullets instead of numbers. Like the ordered list, you apply it using one of the toolbar buttons on the Paragraph Format toolbar. You decide to format your list as an unordered list to see how it appears.

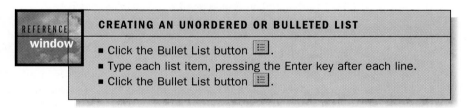

REFERENCE
window

CREATING AN UNORDERED OR BULLETED LIST

- Click the Bullet List button 📋.
- Type each list item, pressing the Enter key after each line.
- Click the Bullet List button 📋.

To format a list as an unordered list:

1. Return to the Netscape Editor.

2. Select the list of attractions by dragging the mouse over all the items in the list.

3. Click the **Bullet List** button 📋 on the Netscape toolbar. The list changes to an unordered list of items as shown in Figure 2-17. Unlike a numbered list, you do not have to view the list in the Netscape browser in order to see the bulleted text.

Figure 2-17 ◀
Creating an
unordered list

unordered list
displays bullets

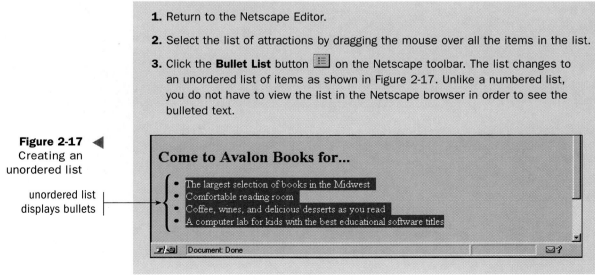

Modifying the Appearance of a List

The Netscape Editor allows you to choose a different symbol for unordered lists or a different numbering format for ordered lists. The bullet symbol is one of the properties of the unordered list style. Some properties, such as the alignment property, can be accessed with toolbar buttons, but not all properties have corresponding toolbar buttons. You access those properties by clicking the selected text with the right mouse button and choosing the appropriate properties option from the popup menu that opens. Clicking with the right mouse button is commonly called **right-clicking**.

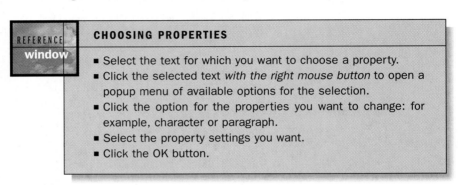

REFERENCE
window

CHOOSING PROPERTIES

- Select the text for which you want to choose a property.
- Click the selected text *with the right mouse button* to open a popup menu of available options for the selection.
- Click the option for the properties you want to change: for example, character or paragraph.
- Select the property settings you want.
- Click the OK button.

You decide to replace the bullet symbol in your list of attractions with a symbol that more closely approximates the square bullet symbol used in the flyer.

To change the bullet symbol:

1. Click the selected unordered list *with the right mouse button* to open the popup menu.

2. Click **Paragraph/List properties** from the popup menu.

3. If necessary, click the **Paragraph** sheet tab.

4. Click the **Bullet style** list arrow ▾, then click **Solid square** from the Bullet style list.

5. Click the **OK** button. The items in the list are now preceded by the new bullet style. See Figure 2-18.

Figure 2-18 ◀
Changing the
bullet style

new bullet style —————

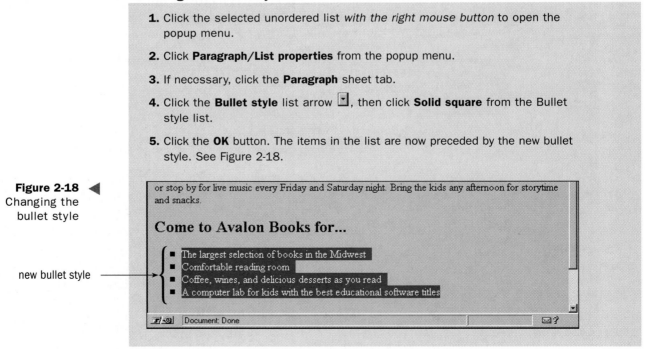

or stop by for live music every Friday and Saturday night. Bring the kids any afternoon for storytime and snacks.

Come to Avalon Books for...

■ The largest selection of books in the Midwest
■ Comfortable reading room
■ Coffee, wines, and delicious desserts as you read
■ A computer lab for kids with the best educational software titles

Document: Done

Indenting Text

If you want to offset text from the left edge of the page, you can do so by indenting the text using the Indent buttons 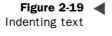 and 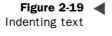 on the toolbar.

Based on Mark's flyer you decide to indent the descriptions of the upcoming events. First you enter the text describing the upcoming events.

To enter the week's events and indent the descriptions:

1. Click the end of the heading "This week's events," then press **Enter**.

> TROUBLE? If you can't see this heading, scroll down the document window.

2. Verify that the Normal style is applied by checking the Paragraph style list box.

> TROUBLE? If the style does not appear as Normal, select the Normal style from the Paragraph style list box.

3. Type **Monday, 10/7**, then press **Enter**.

4. Type the following, then press **Enter**:

Isaac Anderson discusses humor and science fiction and will sign copies of his new book, The Time Traveler's Bar and Grill

5. Continue typing the following information into the document window, pressing **Enter** after each line.

Wednesday, 10/9

The Avalon Reading Club will discuss Maureen Dawson's book, Deconstructing Beethoven

Friday, 10/11

Soft Jazz by Burns, Sutton, and Davis

6. Select the line or lines describing the Isaac Anderson discussion and book signing (do not include the date).

7. Click the **Increase Indent** button to shift the line to the right.

8. Indent the rest of the event descriptions in the list, leaving the dates unindented. Your page should look like Figure 2-19.

Figure 2-19 ◀
Indenting text

indented text ————

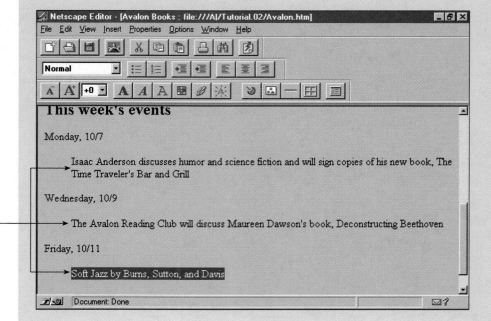

Applying Character Tags

While you can't change the definition of a style like "Heading 1," you can alter the appearance of individual characters. The HTML formats that you can apply to characters are called **character tags**. The Netscape Editor allows you to use character tags to italicize your text, bold it, increase its size, or display it in a different color.

REFERENCE window	**APPLYING CHARACTER TAGS** ■ Select the text to which you want to apply the character tag. ■ Click one of the buttons on the Character Format toolbar.

Changing Font Attributes

A **font attribute** is a characteristic of a font that you can change, including its size, color, and whether it is in bold or italics. Font attributes are represented in the Netscape Editor by toolbar buttons on the Character Format toolbar. You notice from Mark's flyer that the descriptions of the upcoming events include book names that should be italicized.

To italicize text in the Avalon page:

1. Select the text **The Time Traveler's Bar and Grill** from the description of the Isaac Anderson discussion.

2. Click the **Italic** button on the Character Format toolbar.

3. Select the text **Deconstructing Beethoven** from the description of the Reading Club event.

4. Click .

To help the dates stand out better on the page, you decide to bold the day of the event by applying the bold character tag.

To bold text in the Avalon page:

1. Select the text **Monday** from the list of events.

2. Click the **Bold** button on the Character Format toolbar.

3. Repeat steps 1 and 2 to bold Wednesday and Friday. The updated page should appear as shown in Figure 2-20.

Figure 2-20 ◄
Applying
character tags

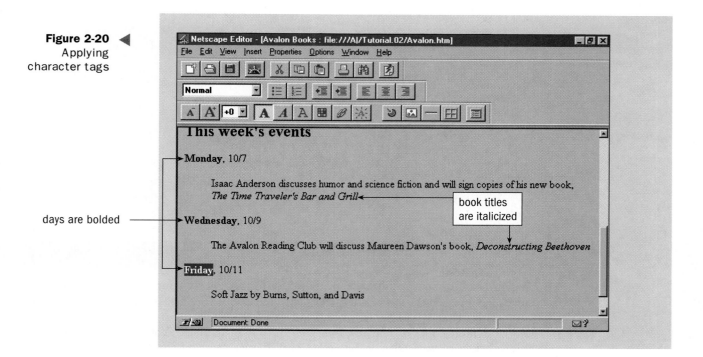

days are bolded ————

Increasing Font Size

Font size is another font attribute you can change. You have already seen how to change the font size of an entire paragraph by applying one of the heading styles. To change the font size of individual characters, not necessarily entire lines or paragraphs, you can use the font size character tag. Because of the nature of HTML, you cannot specify the actual font size for your text. You can't say, "I want this heading to appear in a 14-point size." Remember that it is the browser that determines the appearance of your page. All you can do is specify how big you want the text sized *relative to the Normal style*. The Netscape Editor allows you to specify font sizes ranging from 2 points smaller than the Normal style to 4 points larger.

Looking at your page, you decide to increase the size of the Avalon Books heading. At present it is formatted with the Heading 1 tag. The font size for the Heading 1 tag, as you can see if you click the Heading 1 tag and then look at the value in the Font Size list box, appears as +3—three points larger than the Normal style. You would like the text to be larger, but there isn't another heading tag that will display the text in a larger font. You can increase the font size of the Avalon Books heading by selecting the text and applying a character tag that increases the text size by one point.

To increase the size of the Avalon Books heading:

1. Scroll to the top of your Web page, then select the text **Avalon Books** in the first line of your page.

2. Click the **Increase Font Size** button on the Character Format toolbar. The font size is increased by one point to 4 points larger than Normal text. Figure 2-21 shows the updated page heading.

Figure 2-21 ◀
Increasing
font size

font is four points
larger than normal

Changing Font Color

Another way of adding emphasis and interest to the text on your page is to use different colors by applying the Color character tag to selected text. Netscape allows you to choose colors from a palette of colors or you can define your own.

The default color of text in your Web document is black. You decide to change the color of the first two lines of the page to red to give them greater emphasis.

To change the text color:

1. Select the first two headings on the page.

2. Click the **Font Color** button 🏢 on the Character Format toolbar.

3. Click the **red** color in the first column and second row of the Basic Colors grid. See Figure 2-22.

Figure 2-22 ◀
Changing
font color

click this color

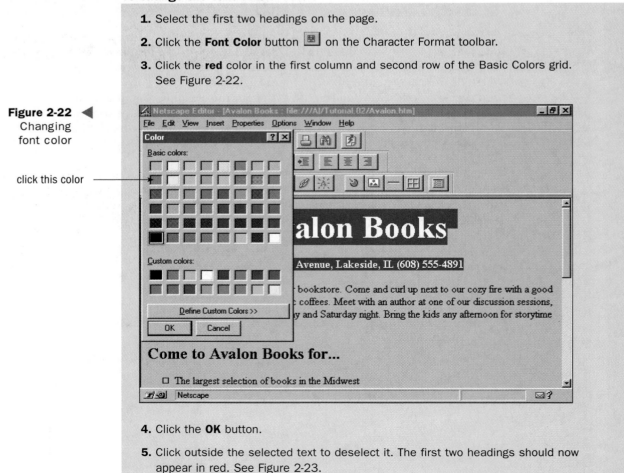

4. Click the **OK** button.

5. Click outside the selected text to deselect it. The first two headings should now appear in red. See Figure 2-23.

Figure 2-23
New font color

text is now red

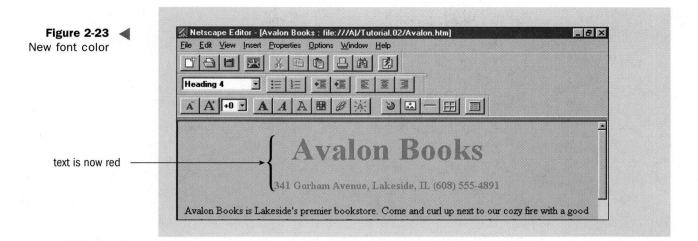

Applying Multiple Character Tags

So far you've been changing one character property at a time using the buttons on the toolbars. You can apply more than one character tag at a time using the Character Properties dialog box. You open this dialog box the way you open any properties dialog box: by right-clicking the selected text and choosing the appropriate properties option from the popup menu that appears. You then make the selections you want in the property sheets, and apply them all at once by clicking the OK button.

Mark stops by and looks at the work you've done. He's pleased with the use of color on the page and would like you to change the color for the two other headings. He thinks they should be italicized as well. You can change the font style, size, and color properties all at the same time using the Character Properties sheet.

To apply multiple character tags using the Character Properties sheet:

1. Select the line **Come to Avalon Books for...**.

2. Right-click the selection, then click **Character properties** from the popup menu.

3. In the Properties dialog box, click the **Italic** check box.

4. Click the **Custom Color** check box, then click the **Choose Color** button.

5. Click the **blue** color box in the first row and sixth column, then click the **OK** button. You leave the size of the font at two points larger than normal. Figure 2-24 shows the completed Properties dialog box.

Figure 2-24 ◄
Setting
character
properties

new blue color

text will be italicized

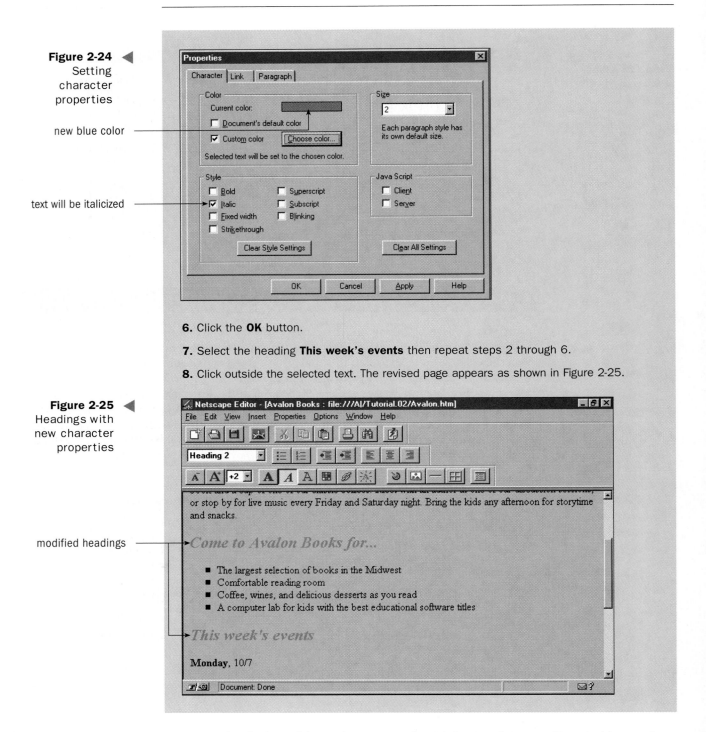

6. Click the **OK** button.

7. Select the heading **This week's events** then repeat steps 2 through 6.

8. Click outside the selected text. The revised page appears as shown in Figure 2-25.

Figure 2-25 ◄
Headings with
new character
properties

modified headings

You're finished modifying the text on the Avalon Books page. You decide to take a break. Save your changes to the file and close all of the Netscape windows. In the next session you'll add graphic elements to the page.

To save your changes and then exit Netscape:

1. Click **File**, then click **Exit**.

2. Click the **Yes** button twice to close all Netscape windows and save your changes. All of your Netscape windows close and your Web page is saved to your Student Disk.

Quick Check

1 How are ordered lists displayed by the Netscape Editor? In the Netscape browser?

2 How do you change the symbol the Netscape Editor uses in unordered lists?

3 What does it mean for text to have a font size of +3 points?

4 How would you change the font size, font color, and appearance for a section of text without opening several dialog boxes?

5 How would you change the color of text on your page to green?

SESSION

2.3

In this session you learn how to insert graphic elements on your page, including graphical lines and pictures. You will also learn how to modify the properties of these graphical elements.

Inserting a Horizontal Line

Part of the popularity of the Web is due to the ability of browsers like Netscape to display graphic objects within the Web page. Graphic objects lend interest to the page and allow Web authors to share visual information. However, because graphic objects require more time than normal text for a browser to access, you should use graphic objects sparingly.

To give shape to your page, consider adding horizontal lines. Horizontal lines divide the Web page into sections for easy viewing.

REFERENCE
window

INSERTING A HORIZONTAL LINE

- Click the end of the paragraph below which you want to insert the line.
- Click the Insert Horizontal Line button ⊟ on the Character Format toolbar.
- To change the line's appearance, right-click the horizontal line and click Horizontal Line properties from the popup menu. Make any changes you want, then click the OK button.

Mark's flyer includes horizontal lines, and he would like his Web page to feature them as well. You decide to add a horizontal line separating the name and address of the bookstore from the rest of the page.

To insert a horizontal line:

1. Restart Netscape Navigator. You do not have to initiate an Internet connection nor load your home page.

2. Click **File**, then click **Open File in Editor**.

3. In the Open dialog box, locate the drive containing your Student Disk, open the **Tutorial.02** folder, then click **Avalon.htm** and click the **Open** button. Your Avalon Books page opens in the Netscape Editor window.

4. Click the end of the heading containing address information for Avalon Books.

5. Click the **Insert Horizontal Line** button ⊟ on the Character Format toolbar.

A horizontal line appears on the page shown in Figure 2-26.

Figure 2-26
Adding a
horizontal line

inserted horizontal
line

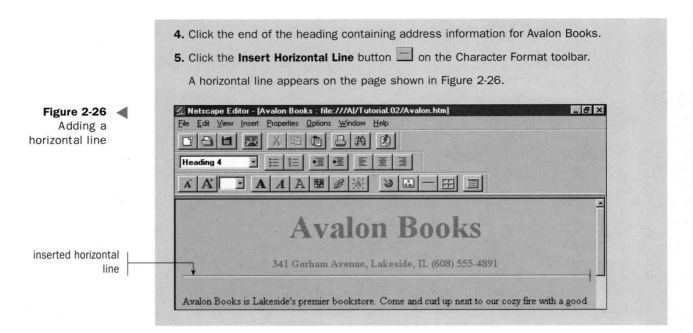

The default horizontal line shown in Figure 2-26 is centered, 2 pixels wide and is formatted with a three-dimensional effect. You can use the Horizontal Line Properties dialog box to change your line's width, height, alignment, and appearance. Figure 2-27 describes the properties you can change.

Figure 2-27
Line properties

Property	Description
Width	The width of the line is expressed either as a percentage of the window or in the number of pixels, where a **pixel** is a single dot or point on your monitor's screen. Therefore, setting the line width to 100% means the line will stretch the full width of the document window. If you want the line to always stretch across the document window, you should use the percent of window option. If you are trying to define the line width so that it is the same for all browsers, you should use the pixels option.
Height	The height of the line is always expressed in pixels, with a default height of two pixels.
Alignment	Lines can be left-, centered, or right-aligned on the page.
3-D Effect	A line can appear with or without a 3-D effect, which gives the line an illusion of depth.

Figure 2-28 shows several examples of lines whose appearance varies depending on the properties they use.

Figure 2-28 ◄
Examples of
line styles

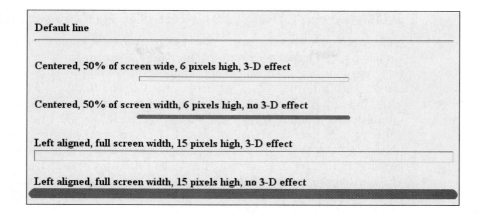

You decide to modify the appearance of the line you just created to make it look more like the one in Mark's flyer.

To change the properties of a horizontal line:

1. Right-click the horizontal line, then click **Horizontal Line properties** from the popup menu.

2. Type **3** in the Height box to set the line's height to three pixels.

3. Type **325** in the Width box and select **Pixels** for the width type.

4. Verify that the **Center** alignment option button is selected.

5. Deselect the **3-D shading** check box. The completed Horizontal Line Properties dialog box should appear as shown in Figure 2-29.

Figure 2-29 ◄
Changing line
properties

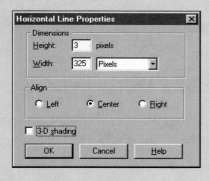

6. Click the **OK** button, then click outside the horizontal line. Figure 2-30 displays the revised horizontal line.

Figure 2-30 ◄
Line with new
properties

revised horizontal line ——

Adding Graphic Images to a Web Page

Most Web browsers can display two types of graphics: inline images and external images. An **inline image** appears directly on the Web page your browser has accessed. To ensure that your inline image is displayable by most browsers, you should use one of two graphic file formats: GIF or JPEG. Of the two, the GIF file format is the more common on the Web, though JPEG graphics are becoming increasingly more common. If you have a graphic in a different format, you should convert it to a GIF or a JPEG file. For example, if you create a graphic in the Windows Paint accessory, you save it as a BMP file. You will need to convert the BMP file using a **graphics converter**, a program that allows you to save graphics in different file formats, before you can use the graphic on your page.

An **external image** is not displayed on the Web page itself. Instead, a link—either a textual or graphical link—appears on the page that represents the image. Figure 2-31 shows the difference between inline and external images.

Figure 2-31
Inline vs.
external
graphic image

inline image appears
on Web page

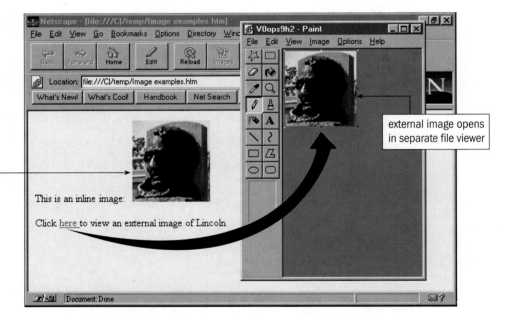

To view an external image, your browser must have a **file viewer**, a program that the browser loads automatically whenever you try to access an external image whose format the browser recognizes. You can find file viewers at several Web sites on the Internet. Whenever Netscape encounters an image type that it does not recognize it prompts you to choose a file viewer for that image. External images have one disadvantage: You can't actually display them on the Web page. Instead, someone reading your page must activate an icon to view the image. However, external images are not limited to the GIF or JPEG formats. You can set up virtually any image format as an external image on a Web page, including video clips and sound files.

GIF File Formats

GIF files come in two formats: interlaced or noninterlaced. When you create your GIF file, you'll need to decide which format you want to use. The difference between the two formats lies in how your browser displays the graphic as it loads the page. With a **noninterlaced** GIF, the image appears one line at a time, starting from the top of the image and working down to the bottom. The effect of this is shown in Figure 2-32. If the graphic is a large one, it might take several minutes for the entire image to appear. People who access your page might find this annoying if the part of the graphic they are interested in is located at the bottom.

Figure 2-32
Noninterlaced
image as
browser
retrieves it

top appears first

image appears one
line at a time

entire image is
retrieved

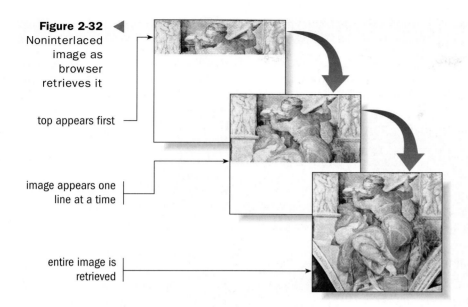

With an **interlaced** GIF, the image appears "stepwise." For example, every fifth line might appear first, followed by every sixth line, and so forth through the remaining rows. As shown in Figure 2-33, the effect of interlacing is that the graphic starts out as a blurry representation of the final image, only gradually coming into focus.

Figure 2-33
Interlaced
image as
browser
retrieves it

a rough image
appears first

image starts to show
more detail

final image is crisp
and detailed

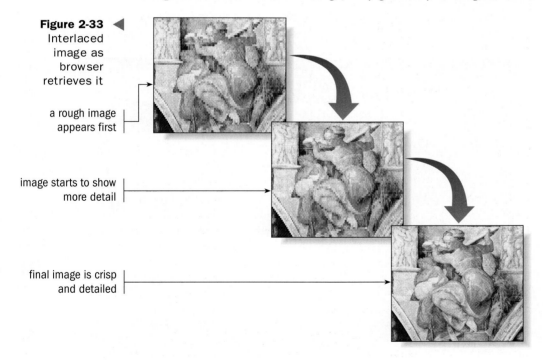

A noninterlaced graphic is always sharp but incomplete while the browser retrieves it. Interlacing is an effective format if you have a large image and want to give users a preview of the final image. They get an idea of what it looks like and can decide whether they want to wait for it to "come into focus." If you are using a graphics package to create GIF images for your Web page, you should determine whether it allows you to save the image as an interlaced GIF.

Inserting an Inline Image

Mark has given you the image file he used in the Avalon Books flyer. You have converted it to a GIF file with one of your graphics programs. You are now ready to insert the graphic into the Avalon Books Web page.

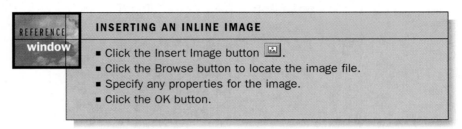

REFERENCE window

INSERTING AN INLINE IMAGE

- Click the Insert Image button 🖻.
- Click the Browse button to locate the image file.
- Specify any properties for the image.
- Click the OK button.

To insert an inline image:

1. Click the beginning of the opening paragraph describing the bookstore to place the insertion point.

2. Click the **Insert Image** button 🖻 on the Character Format toolbar. The Properties dialog box opens to the Image sheet tab.

3. Click the **Browse** button next to the File name box, then locate and select the **Book.gif** file located in the **Tutorial.02** folder on your Student Disk.

4. Click the **Open** button, then click the **OK** button. The book graphic is inserted onto the page as shown in Figure 2-34.

Figure 2-34 ◀
Inserted
graphic

graphic ⟶

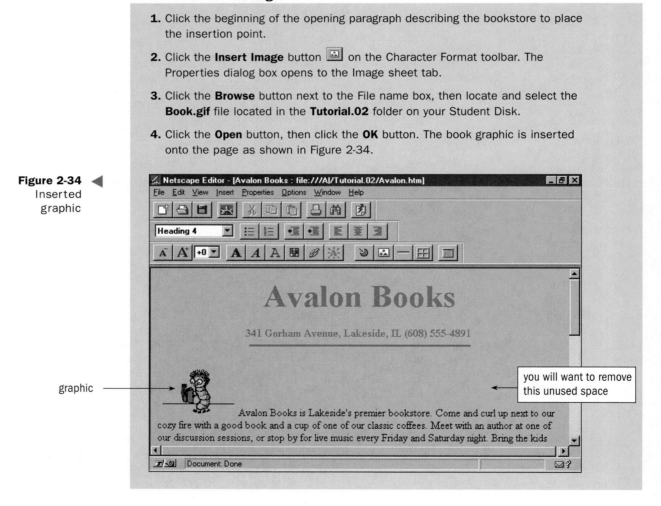

you will want to remove this unused space

Setting Image Properties

The Netscape Editor gives you some control over how the image appears on your page. You can change the size of the image, add a border, change the distance between the graphic and surrounding text, and modify how the graphic is aligned relative to surrounding text.

As shown in Figure 2-35, the Netscape Editor gives you seven options to specify how the graphic and text are aligned. You can align the text surrounding the graphic with the graphic's top, center, or bottom. You can also have surrounding text wrapped to the left or the right of the image.

Figure 2-35 ◄
Examples of
aligned text

Alignment	Appearance
Text aligned with top of graphic	 Avalon Books is Lakeside's premier bookstore. Come and curl up next to our cozy fire with a good book and a cup of one of our classic coffees. Meet with an author at one of our discussion sessions, or stop by for live music every Friday and Saturday night. Bring the kids any afternoon for storytime and snacks.
Text aligned with bottom of graphic	 Avalon Books is Lakeside's premier bookstore. Come and curl up next to our cozy fire with a good book and a cup of one of our classic coffees. Meet with an author at one of our discussion sessions, or stop by for live music every Friday and Saturday night. Bring the kids any afternoon for storytime and snacks.
Text wrapped to the left of graphic	Avalon Books is Lakeside's premier bookstore. Come and curl up next to our cozy fire with a good book and a cup of one of our classic coffees. Meet with an author at one of our discussion sessions, or stop by for live music every Friday and Saturday night. Bring the kids any afternoon for storytime and snacks. 
Text aligned with center of graphic	 Avalon Books is Lakeside's premier bookstore. Come and curl up next to our cozy fire with a good book and a cup of one of our classic coffees. Meet with an author at one of our discussion sessions, or stop by for live music every Friday and Saturday night. Bring the kids any afternoon for storytime and snacks.
Text wrapped to the right of graphic	 Avalon Books is Lakeside's premier bookstore. Come and curl up next to our cozy fire with a good book and a cup of one of our classic coffees. Meet with an author at one of our discussion sessions, or stop by for live music every Friday and Saturday night. Bring the kids any afternoon for storytime and snacks.

For large graphics you can use the Netscape Editor to specify alternative images for the graphic. An **alternative image** is an image that gives users something to look at as they wait for the browser to finish retrieving the larger image from the Web server. You can also specify that text will appear as a browser retrieves a graphic image. This is useful for users who are accessing your page with a text browser incapable of displaying the image. In those cases, they can still read your text description.

Another option to consider for your graphic is the space between the graphic and the surrounding text. As shown in Figure 2-36 you can set up your page to have the text closely hugging the graphic or you can add extra space between the image and the text.

Figure 2-36 ◀
Spacing
between image
and text

less space between
graphic and text

more space between
graphic and text

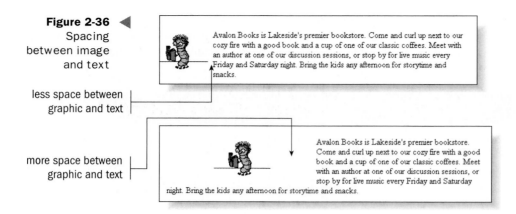

Considering these various options for your graphic, you decide to wrap the paragraph around the graphic you just inserted. This will remove much of the blank space between the horizontal line and the start of the paragraph. You also decide to add space between the graphic and the text in the paragraph. Finally, since the graphic is already small, you feel you do not need to have an alternative representation, but you will include a text description for users who have text browsers.

To modify the properties of an inline image:

1. Click the inline image and click the **Object Properties** button 🔳 on the Character Format toolbar.

2. Type **Come to Avalon Books!** in the Text box in the Alternative representations area.

3. In the Alignment section, click the button that wraps text to the right 🔲.

4. Type **5** in the Left and right box to increase the space around the image to five pixels. The completed dialog box should look like Figure 2-37.

Figure 2-37 ◀
Modifying inline
image
properties

click to wrap text
to the right

five pixels between
image and space

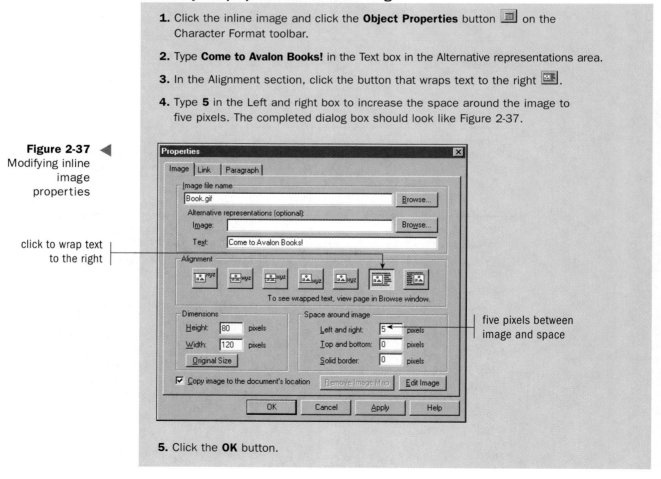

5. Click the **OK** button.

You can't see the effect of wrapping text around an image in the Netscape Editor—instead you must view the page with the Netscape browser. You decide to save your changes to the page and view it there.

To view your changes in the browser:

1. Click the **Save** button 🖫 on the File/Edit toolbar.

2. Click the **View in Browser** button 🖾. Figure 2-38 displays the revised Avalon page.

Figure 2-38 ◀
Inline image in
browser

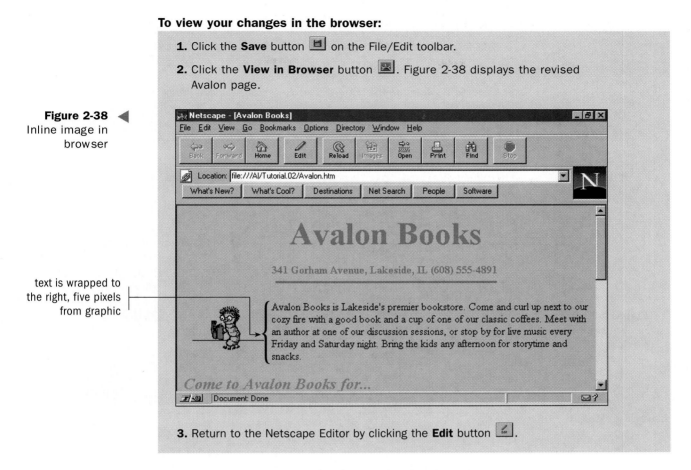

text is wrapped to
the right, five pixels
from graphic

3. Return to the Netscape Editor by clicking the **Edit** button 🖉.

Setting Background Properties

The Netscape Editor allows you to specify a particular color for your background or a particular background image. When you use a graphic as your background, it appears over and over in a pattern across the document window. Many Web pages employ interesting background images to great effect. You should, however, be careful to minimize the size of the graphic image you use. A large graphic image will cause your page to take much longer to load, causing some users to cancel the page before even getting a chance to view it. Generally the size of a graphic used for a page background should not exceed 30 kilobytes. You should also be careful not to let the background image overwhelm the text.

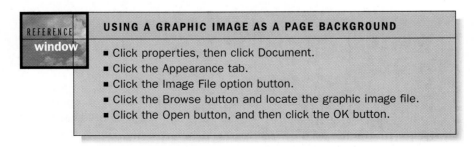

REFERENCE
window

USING A GRAPHIC IMAGE AS A PAGE BACKGROUND

- Click properties, then click Document.
- Click the Appearance tab.
- Click the Image File option button.
- Click the Browse button and locate the graphic image file.
- Click the Open button, and then click the OK button.

You've created an image for the Avalon Books background using the store logo. You've been careful to make the image small and unobtrusive.

To change the background of your Web page:

1. Click **Properties**, then click **Document** to open the Document Properties dialog box.

2. Click the **Appearance** tab.

3. Click the **Browse for File** button in the Background image group box and locate the file **AB.gif** in the Tutorial.02 folder on your Student Disk.

4. Click the **Open** button, then click the **OK** button.

The page is finished. Save the page to your Student Disk and view the final version in the Netscape browser.

To view the final version of your work:

1. Click the **Save** button 🔲.

2. Return to the Netscape browser displaying the Avalon Books page and click the **Reload** button. Figure 2-39 displays the final version of the page.

Figure 2-39 ◀
Final Avalon
Books page in
browser
window

background graphic
displayed in a pattern

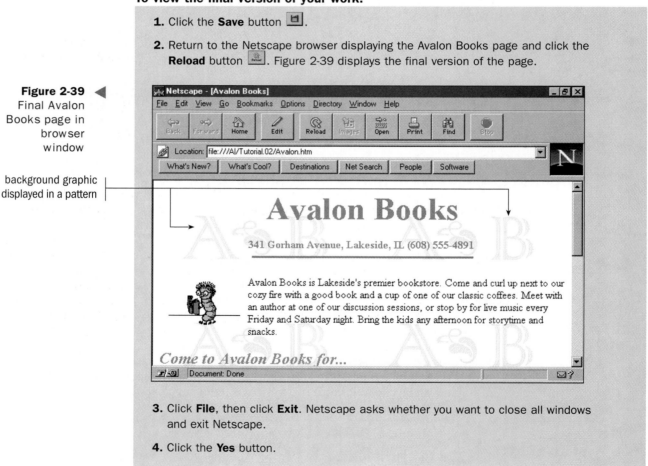

3. Click **File**, then click **Exit**. Netscape asks whether you want to close all windows and exit Netscape.

4. Click the **Yes** button.

You show Mark the final version of the page. He's pleased with the work you've done and will contact his Internet Service Provider about posting this page on the store's Internet account. Since you've done such a good job creating this page, he asks that you be responsible for keeping the page up to date. Since creating the page was so easy with the Netscape Editor, you quickly agree.

Quick Check

1. What is the difference between an inline graphic and an external graphic?

2. What are the only two file formats that can be used for inline graphics?

3. What is the difference between an interlaced graphic and a noninterlaced graphic?

4. How would you set up a horizontal line so that it is centered on a page and covers 25% of the width of the document window?

5. Why should you be careful in wrapping text around a graphic image in your Web document?

6. What should you watch out for when using a graphic image for your page background?

Tutorial Assignments

It's been a week since you created the Avalon Books Web page. Mark approaches you with a list of things he wants to have added and changed on the page. In the upcoming week, the bookstore will host the following events:

Monday, 10/14

A lecture given by Professor Patricia Fuller on *The Art of Maurice Sendak*

Thursday, 10/17

Peter Daynes will sign copies of his new book, *Glencoe Memories*

Friday, 10/18

Classical music by the Lakeside Quartet

Mark asks you to add these events to the page and remove the old event list. He also wants you to include a new item in the bulleted list of Avalon Books attractions: "An impressive collection of used and out-of-print books."

As for the appearance of the page, he wants you to change the color of the activity days so that they match the blue color of the section heading. He also has a new graphic image that he wants you to use in place of the book and quill pen image. He has the image stored in a file called "Book2.gif." When inserting the image he wants you to increase the space between the graphic image and the text in the surrounding paragraph. Finally you should replace the background image with the new Avalon Books logo, found in the "AB2.gif" file. The final version of this page should appear as shown in Figure 2-40.

Figure 2-40 ◀

Avalon Books

341 Gorham Avenue, Lakeside, IL (608) 555-4891

Avalon Books is Lakeside's premier bookstore. Come and curl up next to our cozy fire with a good book and a cup of one of our classic coffees. Meet with an author at one of our discussion sessions, or stop by for live music every Friday and Saturday night. Bring the kids any afternoon for storytime and snacks.

Come to Avalon Books for...

- The largest selection of books in the Midwest
- Comfortable reading rooms
- Coffe, wines and delicious desserts as you read
- A computer lab for kids with the best educational software titles
- An impressive collection of used and out-of-print books

This week's events

Monday, 10/14

A lecture given by Professor Patricia Fuller on *The Art of Maurice Sendak*

Thursday, 10/17

Peter Daynes will sign copies of his new book, *Glencoe Memories*

Friday 10/18

Classical music by the Lakeside Quartet

To complete this tutorial assignment:

1. Open the "Avalon.htm" file that you created in this tutorial in the Netscape Editor.
2. Save the page as "Avalon2" to the TAssign folder on your Student Disk.
3. Change the title located on the General dialog sheet in the Document Properties dialog box to "Avalon Books 2." Type your name in the Author text box and change the description box to read "This is the revised version of the Avalon Books home page."
4. Add the item, "An impressive collection of used and out-of-print books" to the end of the bulleted list.
5. Delete the outdated events list and replace it with the new events list. Use the same indentation.
6. Change the color of the day to match the color of the section heading.
7. Replace the "Book.gif" graphic with the "Book2.gif" graphic found in the TAssign folder of the Tutorial.02 folder on your Student Disk.
8. Change the left/right spacing around the graphic to 9 pixels but continue to wrap the paragraph to the right around the graphic.
9. Replace the "AB.gif" background graphic with the "AB2.gif" graphic in the TAssign folder of the Tutorial.02 folder on your Student Disk.
10. Save the Web page.

11. View the revised page in the Netscape browser. Print out a copy of the page for your instructor.
12. Hand in the printout to your instructor.

Case Problems

1. Creating a Web Page for the River Bar Seafood Restaurant You work as a manager at the River Bar Seafood Restaurant in Woolworth, Missouri. The owner, Gwen Foucoult, has asked you to create a Web page listing the weekly specials at the restaurant. She shows you a printout of what she wants on the page, shown in Figure 2-41.

Figure 2-41 ◀

The River Bar Seafood Restaurant
211 West State St., Woolworth, 555-4532

Stop by the River Bar for the best in seafood, or call us today and order one of our delicious dishes for carryout!

This Week's Specials

Grilled Norwegian Salmon
Grilled salmon topped with Dijon mustard sauce, served with vegetables and roasted red potatoes. $15.95

Grilled Yellowfin Tuna
Grilled and topped with cilantro-lime salsa. Served with roasted red potatoes and vegetables. $15.95

Scallops with Linguine
Jumbo scallops with mushroom and herbs in lemon cream sauce. $14.95

Butterflied Shrimp
Tender shrimp lightly breaded and fried, served with vegetable and rice pilaf. $15.25

Grilled Halibut
Atlantic halibut steak seasoned with lemon and pepper and grilled, served with vegetables and roasted potatoes. $14.95

Using Figure 2-41 as a guide, create the River Bar page.
To complete this case problem:
1. Open the Netscape Editor to a blank page.
2. Enter properties for your document, giving the page the title, "River Bar Specials."
3. Enter your name as the page author.
4. Type "Weekly specials at the River Bar seafood restaurant" in the Description box.
5. Save the page as "Seafood.htm" to the Cases folder in the Tutorial.02 folder on your Student Disk.
6. Enter the text shown in Figure 2-41.
7. Format the main heading using the Heading 2 style.
8. Format the restaurant address using the Heading 5 style.
9. Insert a horizontal line after the restaurant address. Use the default line style.
10. Enter a brief description of the restaurant in the Normal style.
11. Format the heading, "This Week's Specials" with the Heading 3 style.
12. Format the name of each dish with the Heading 4 style.
13. Indent the description of each dish.
14. Use the graphic file "Fish.gif," located in the Cases folder of the Tutorial.02 folder on your Student Disk, as a background for your page.
15. Save your changes to the page.
16. Print out the page and hand in the printout to your instructor.

2. Displaying a Lecture Outline You are the teaching assistant for history professor, Clifford Foote. Starting with this semester, he is putting his lecture outlines on the Web for students to view. He wants you to create the lecture outline for his September 22 lecture on Abraham Lincoln's life prior to the Civil War.

To create such a page you will have to use ordered lists. With the Netscape Editor you specify the symbol used for the list items. You can use Roman Numerals (I, II, III, IV...), capital letters (A,B,C...), numbers (1,2,3...), and so forth. For Professor Foote's lecture outline, you will format major points with the Roman Numerals format. You will also indent minor points, listing them with capital letters.

The professor also has a photo from the Lincoln mausoleum that he wants you to place on the page. The photo has been saved to the file "Lincoln.gif."

The page should include a heading for the history course, the professor's name, and the date of the lecture. The professor also wants you to place the text on a solid blue background. The complete Web page should look like Figure 2-42.

Figure 2-42 ◀

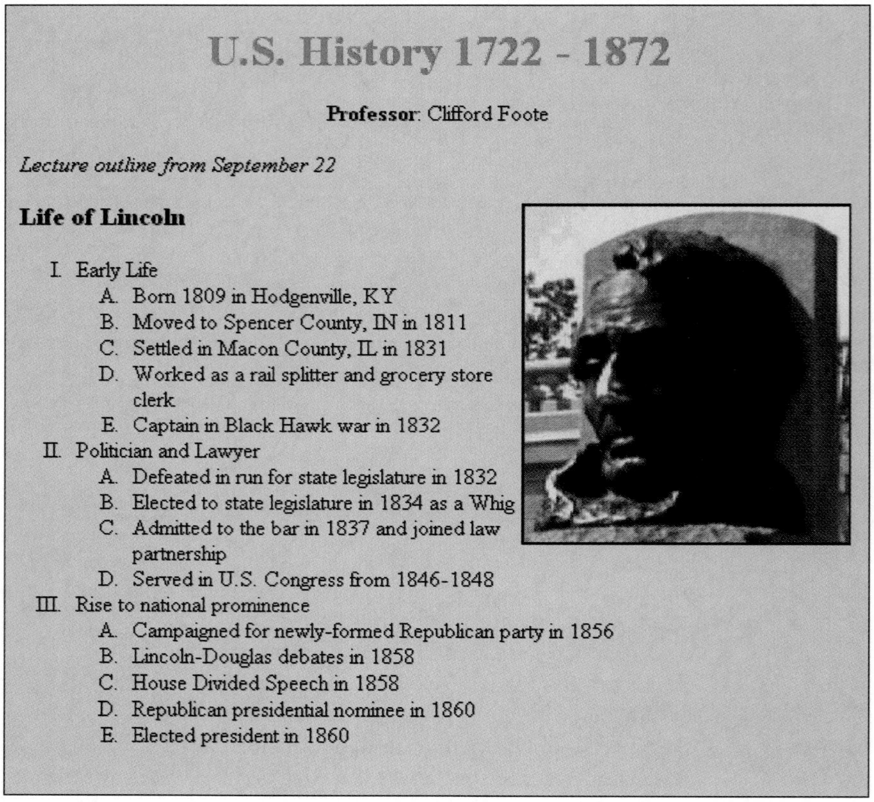

U.S. History 1722 - 1872

Professor: Clifford Foote

Lecture outline from September 22

Life of Lincoln

I. Early Life
    A. Born 1809 in Hodgenville, KY
    B. Moved to Spencer County, IN in 1811
    C. Settled in Macon County, IL in 1831
    D. Worked as a rail splitter and grocery store clerk
    E. Captain in Black Hawk war in 1832
II. Politician and Lawyer
    A. Defeated in run for state legislature in 1832
    B. Elected to state legislature in 1834 as a Whig
    C. Admitted to the bar in 1837 and joined law partnership
    D. Served in U.S. Congress from 1846-1848
III. Rise to national prominence
    A. Campaigned for newly-formed Republican party in 1856
    B. Lincoln-Douglas debates in 1858
    C. House Divided Speech in 1858
    D. Republican presidential nominee in 1860
    E. Elected president in 1860

To complete this case problem:

1. Open a blank document in the Netscape Editor.
2. On the General tab of the Document Properties dialog box, type "September 22 lecture" in the Title box.
3. Type your name in the Properties Author box.
4. Type "The outline of the 9/22 lecture in U.S. history" in the Description box.
5. Set the page background color to blue (first row, fifth column in the list of basic colors).
6. Save the page as "Lincoln.htm" to the Cases folder in the Tutorial.02 folder on your Student Disk.
7. Type the main heading "U.S. History 1722-1872," formatted with the Heading 1 style and centered on the page.
8. Change the color of the main heading to red (second row, first column in the list of basic colors).

9. Type the secondary heading "Professor: Clifford Foote," formatted with the Normal style and centered.
10. Bold the title of professor.
11. Type "Lecture outline from September 22," formatted with the Normal style, italicized, and left-aligned.
12. Type "Life of Lincoln," formatted with the Heading 3 style and left-aligned.

13. Enter the three main outline heads as an ordered list, and use the Roman Numeral style for the list items.
14. Within each main point, enter the subpoints as an ordered list using the Capital Letter style for each item.
15. Indent the subpoints.
16. At the beginning of the line reading "Life of Lincoln" insert the "Lincoln.gif" image, available in the Cases folder of the Tutorial.02 folder on your Student Disk.
17. Format the image so that text will wrap around the image on the left.
18. Add a 2 pixel width border to the image.
19. Save your completed page.
20. View the page in the Netscape browser and print the page.
21. Hand in the printout to your instructor.

3. Using Preformatted Text on the Weber State Weather Page One characteristic of HTML is that it does not allow you to do formatting outside of the formatting options specified by tags. For example, you can't type in two blank spaces in a row (try it!). This can cause problems when you have to insert text in which the alignment of characters is crucial. Consider the temperature chart shown in Figure 2-43.

Figure 2-43 ◀

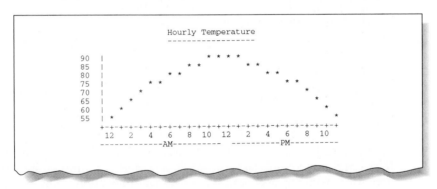

You are in charge of a weather page at Weber State University. You use a program that creates temperature charts like the one shown in Figure 2-43. As part of the daily updates to your Web page, you have to place the new temperature chart on the page. However, the chart as it appears cannot be typed in. You can get around limitations in HTML by using another of the styles provided with the Netscape Editor called "formatted." The **formatted tag** shows text "as is," including any extra spaces. The temperature chart has been placed in the file "Temp.txt" in the Cases folder of the Tutorial.02 folder on your Student Disk. By copying the temperature chart from the Temp.txt file and pasting it into the Netscape Editor, try to create a Web page detailing the previous day's temperature variations.

To complete this case problem:

1. Open the Netscape Editor to a blank page.
2. Open the Document Properties dialog box to the General sheet.
3. Type "Weber State Weather Page" as the title of the page.
4. Enter your name in the Author box.
5. Type "This page displays a temperature chart from the previous day" in the Description box.
6. Save the page as "Temp" in the Cases folder in the Tutorial.02 folder on your Student Disk.
7. Return to the document window and type the text "Yesterday's Temperature Chart" at the top of the page.

8. Format the heading with the Heading 1 style and center it on the page.
9. Beneath the heading, type yesterday's date.
10. Center the date and format it with the Heading 5 style.
11. Insert a horizontal line beneath the date.
12. Open the file "Temp.txt" in the Cases folder of the Tutorial.02 folder on your Student Disk with your text word processor (Windows users can use Notepad).
13. Copy the temperature chart.
14. Return to the Temp page.

15. Insert a new paragraph underneath the horizontal line and format it with the Formatted tag on the Paragraph style list.
16. Click the Left Align button to align any Formatted text with the left edge of the window.

17. Paste the temperature chart into the new line.
18. Save the changes you made to the Temp page.
19. View the page in the Netscape browser.
20. Print the page and hand in the printout to your instructor.

4. Creating a Realty Listing You work as a realty agent for TK Realty. Just recently your company has started putting listings on the World Wide Web. You're responsible for creating your own listing. One of the houses you want to create a Web page for is a lakefront house located at 22 Northshore Drive. The owners have given you this description that they want placed on the page:

"This is a must see. Large waterfront home overlooking Lake Mills. It comes complete with 3 bedrooms, a huge master bedroom, hot tub, family room, large office, and three-car garage. Wood boat ramp. Great condition."

The main points about the house are:

- 2300 sq. feet
- 15 years old
- Updated electrical and heat
- Asking price: $230,000

You also have a photo of the house, saved as "House.jpg" in the Cases folder on the Tutorial.02 folder on your Student Disk. Using this information, create a page describing the house to interested house-hunters. You may choose any design for the page, but it must include the following elements:

1. a title, description, and your name in the Document Properties sheet
2. a main heading
3. the photo of the house
4. a bulleted list describing the features of the house
5. a paragraph containing the owner's description
6. information on how to contact you, in italics

Save the page you create in the cases folder on the Tutorial.02 folder on your Student Disk with the name "Realty."

Creating a Hypertext Document

Creating a Web Presentation

CASE

The Findlay Farmhouse Bed and Breakfast

Prince Edward Island in Canada is a popular summer vacation spot. The island is known for its natural beauty and peaceful setting. Visitors to the island can choose their lodging from several attractive inns and picturesque bed and breakfasts. One of the most popular bed and breakfasts on the island is the Findlay Farmhouse outside of Summerside. The proprietors, Ian and Fiona Findlay, have owned the inn for many years. Several years ago they bought a computer to help manage their business, and recently they set up an Internet connection. The Findlays want to advertise their bed and breakfast on the Internet in hopes that it will generate new business. Fiona has started creating a page for the Findlay Farmhouse, and she hopes you can help finish it.

Fiona explains that she has organized information about the Findlay Farmhouse and its surroundings into five topics, each with a Heading 2 style heading, with the following titles:

- Your home on Prince Edward Island
- What are they saying about us?
- Area attractions
- How do I get there?
- For more information...

Fiona tells you that she has also created two supplementary Web pages, Bio and Events, that contain information on the Findlay family and area events. She would like users to be able to access the Bio and Events pages from the Findlay Farmhouse page. She would also like users to be able to jump to other pages on Prince Edward Island from the Findlay Farmhouse page, and to be able to send her e-mail messages. You tell her she can accomplish all this with hypertext links. Then you suggest that she could make her page, which is rather long, more user-friendly by adding links that help users move more easily around the page. Fiona agrees that would be a good idea, so the two of you get to work.

In this session you'll learn how to create targets within your Web documents and to create hypertext links to those targets.

Setting Targets

In Tutorial 1 you learned that a hypertext document contains links that you can select, usually by clicking a mouse, to jump instantly to another location, often called the **destination** of the link. In addition to making access to other documents easy, hypertext links provide some important organizational benefits.

For example, when your Web page is too long to fit on a single screen, you can help users quickly locate the information they need by providing hypertext links to important points within the page. A typical screen can display only a small section of a long page— and this could be a problem for users in a hurry. Because many Web users glance at a page and then move on, you should make your page's topics as accessible as possible. You can do this by placing links at the beginning that point to the main topics on the page. When readers click the link, they jump to that section of the document.

To create links that jump to a specific point on a Web page, you must first insert a target at the destination location. A **target**, also called an **anchor**, is a reference point that identifies a specific location on the page. Once you have inserted a target, you have a way of referring to that location. You then create the link and indicate the target to which the link points. Figure 3-1 illustrates how the target you create will work as a reference point for a link.

Figure 3-1 ◄
Link pointing
to a target
within the
same Web
document

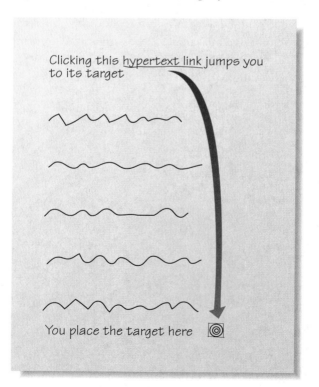

Clicking this hypertext link jumps you to its target

You place the target here ◎

Targets do not appear in the browser, but you can view them in the Netscape Editor. Targets don't have to be just text. You can also designate inline images to act as targets.

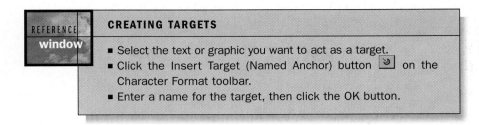

REFERENCE window

CREATING TARGETS

- Select the text or graphic you want to act as a target.
- Click the Insert Target (Named Anchor) button 🔲 on the Character Format toolbar.
- Enter a name for the target, then click the OK button.

For the Findlay Web page, you decide to create five targets—one target at each of the five section headings of the document. You can then create links at the beginning of the page that point to each of the five targets. A user can click one of the links to jump to its target without having to scroll through the page to reach it. Figure 3-2 shows the location of the five targets you will create on the Findlay Web page.

Figure 3-2
Targets in the Findlay Web page

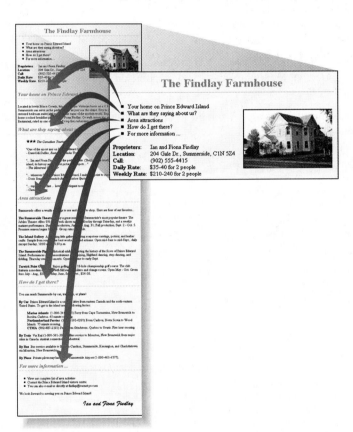

Fiona stored her page as Findlay.htm. You'll open the file and save it with a new name, Findlay2.htm, so you can work with the original later if you want.

To open the Findlay.htm file in the Netscape Editor and save it with a new name:

1. Double-click the **Netscape Navigator** icon 🔲 on your computer's desktop or within the Netscape program window.

2. If your computer tries to initiate an Internet connection, click the **Cancel** button. You do not need an Internet connection to use the Netscape Editor.

3. If the Netscape browser tries to load a home page, click the **Stop** button 🔲.

4. Click **File**, then click **Open File in Editor**.

5. Locate and open the **Findlay** file from the Tutorial.03 folder on your Student Disk.

6. Click **File**, then click **Save As**.

7. Type **Findlay2** in the File name box, then click the **Save** button.

8. Scroll down the entire page to view the location of the five section headings.

First you will create the five targets. The Netscape Editor makes it very easy for you to create a target. The first target you create will be for the heading "Your home on Prince Edward Island."

To set a target in your Web page:

1. Scroll the page to the first section heading, "Your home on Prince Edward Island." Make sure you are viewing the section heading, not the bulleted list.

2. Click at the start of the section heading to place the blinking insertion point at the beginning of the line.

TROUBLE? If you click too far to the left of the section heading, you highlight the heading. Make sure the blinking insertion point is just to the left of the heading, as shown in Figure 3-3.

3. Click the **Insert Target (Named Anchor)** button 🔖 on the Character Format toolbar.

TROUBLE? If you don't see the Character Format toolbar, you can also click the Target (Named Anchor) option on the Insert menu.

4. Type **Your home** in the target name text box as shown in Figure 3-3.

Figure 3-3 ◀
Setting a target

Insert Target (Named Anchor) button

click here to insert target

target name

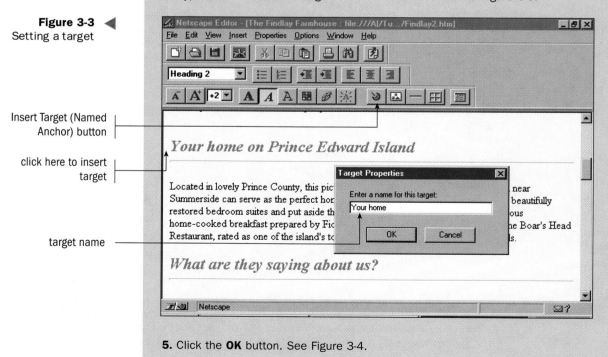

5. Click the **OK** button. See Figure 3-4.

Figure 3-4 ◀
Target in
Netscape
Editor

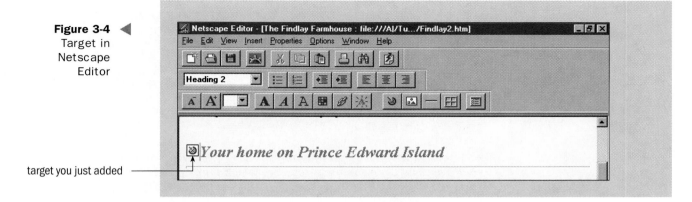

target you just added —

The target icon 🔯 indicates the presence of a target on a Web page. This icon appears only in the Netscape Editor—not in the browser. If you ever forget the name you gave the target, you can view the name in the status bar as you pass your mouse pointer over the target icon.

You're ready to add the rest of the targets, one for each section heading. You can type in any characters or blanks spaces into the target name. Be sure you pay attention to case. A target named "home" is different from one named "HOME."

To add your other hypertext targets:

1. Scroll down to the heading, "What are they saying about us?" then click the left side of the heading.

2. Click the **Insert Target (Named Anchor)** button 🔯 and type **Reviews**, then click the **OK** button.

3. Scroll down to the heading, "Area attractions," then click the left side of the heading.

4. Add a target named **Attractions**.

5. Scroll down to the heading, "How do I get there?" then add a target named **Travel**.

6. Scroll down to the heading, "For more information," then add a target named **More Info**. Now all five targets are in place. You are ready to create hypertext links to the targets.

Hypertext Links

With the Netscape Editor you can insert links into a Web page either by turning existing text into a hypertext link or by inserting linked text directly into the page.

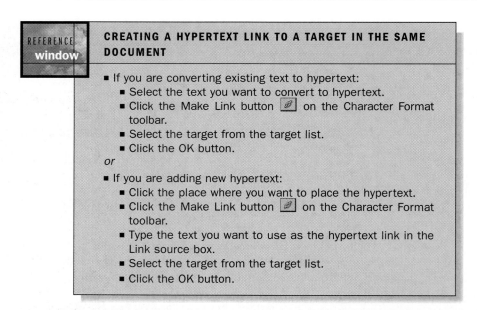

CREATING A HYPERTEXT LINK TO A TARGET IN THE SAME DOCUMENT

- If you are converting existing text to hypertext:
  - Select the text you want to convert to hypertext.
  - Click the Make Link button 🖉 on the Character Format toolbar.
  - Select the target from the target list.
  - Click the OK button.

  or

- If you are adding new hypertext:
  - Click the place where you want to place the hypertext.
  - Click the Make Link button 🖉 on the Character Format toolbar.
  - Type the text you want to use as the hypertext link in the Link source box.
  - Select the target from the target list.
  - Click the OK button.

Changing Existing Text to Hypertext

You can change existing text to a hypertext link by simply selecting the text, then clicking the Make Link button 🖉 and indicating the target to which you want the link to point. The Findlay Farmhouse page begins with a bulleted list that corresponds to the five section headings. By changing the items in this list to hypertext links, you enable users to jump directly to a target. You begin by creating the link to the first section heading, which has a target named Your home.

To change the list item to a hypertext link:

1. Scroll to the top of the page.

2. Select **Your home on Prince Edward Island** from the bulleted list.

3. Click the **Make Link** button 🖉 on the Character Format toolbar.

   TROUBLE? If you don't see the Character Format toolbar, you can also select the Make Link option on the Insert menu.

4. If necessary, click the **Link** tab.

5. Click **Your home** from the list of named targets in the current document. Figure 3-5 shows the completed dialog box.

Figure 3-5 ◄
Selecting a target for a hypertext link

existing text on page will be converted to hypertext link

pound sign appears before target name, indicating it is a target

target list

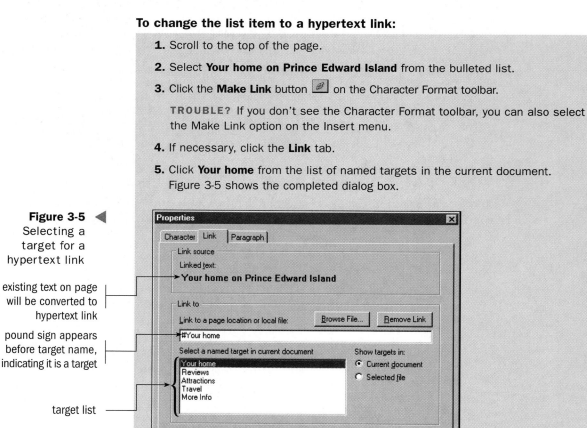

6. Click the **OK** button, then click the page to deselect the link. The text, "Your home on Prince Edward Island," is now underlined and in a different color as shown in Figure 3-6, indicating that it is a hypertext link.

Figure 3-6 ◀
Hypertext link
you just added

hypertext link ───────

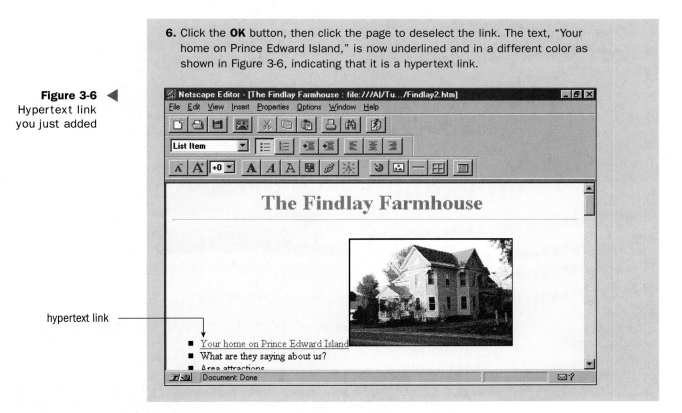

You can confirm the location of a hypertext link in the Netscape Editor by moving your mouse pointer over the linked text. The link's target appears in the status bar. Note that the name of the target is prefaced by a pound sign (#). All target names are prefaced by this symbol to differentiate them from other names such as file names or document locations.

Using the same technique you just learned, turn the other items in the bulleted list to hypertext links.

To convert the rest of the list to hypertext links:

1. Select the list item, **What are they saying about us?** then link the text to the **Reviews** target.

2. Select the list item, **Area attractions**, then link the text to the **Attractions** target.

3. Select the list item, **How do I get there?** then link the text to the **Travel** target.

4. Select the list item, **For more information...**, then link the text to the **More Info** target. Figure 3-7 shows the completed list of hypertext links.

Figure 3-7 ◀
Inserted links

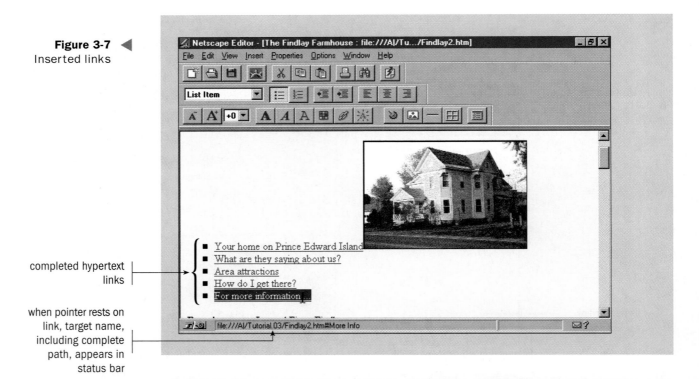

completed hypertext
links

when pointer rests on
link, target name,
including complete
path, appears in
status bar

Inserting New Hypertext Links

Although the Findlay Farmhouse page had a list of topics already there for you to convert to hypertext, often you'll want to create a new link from scratch. For example, you
notice that there is no easy way of returning to the top of the Findlay Farmhouse page,
aside from the scrolling. You realize that it might be helpful to include a hypertext link
pointing to the top of the page. This is a common feature of very long pages. To create
this hypertext link, you first must create a target at the top of the page.

To add a target to the top of the page:

1. If necessary, scroll to the top of the document, then click to the left of the main
   heading, **The Findlay Farmhouse**.

2. Click the **Insert Target (Named Anchor)** button 🔖 .

3. Type **Top** in the target name box, then click the **OK** button.

Now you create a new hypertext link at the bottom of the document that points to the
target you just created at the top of the page. You can enter the link text directly from the
Link Properties dialog box.

To insert hypertext into the document:

1. Scroll down to the bottom of the page.

2. Click at the end of the line: **We look forward to meeting you on Prince Edward
   Island!** then press **Enter**.

3. Click the **Make Link** button 🔗 .

4. Click **Top** from the list of targets.

5. Click the **Enter text to display for new link** box, then type **Return to the top of
   the page.** See Figure 3-8.

Figure 3-8 ◀
Entering text
for a new link

this text will appear
as a hypertext link

target

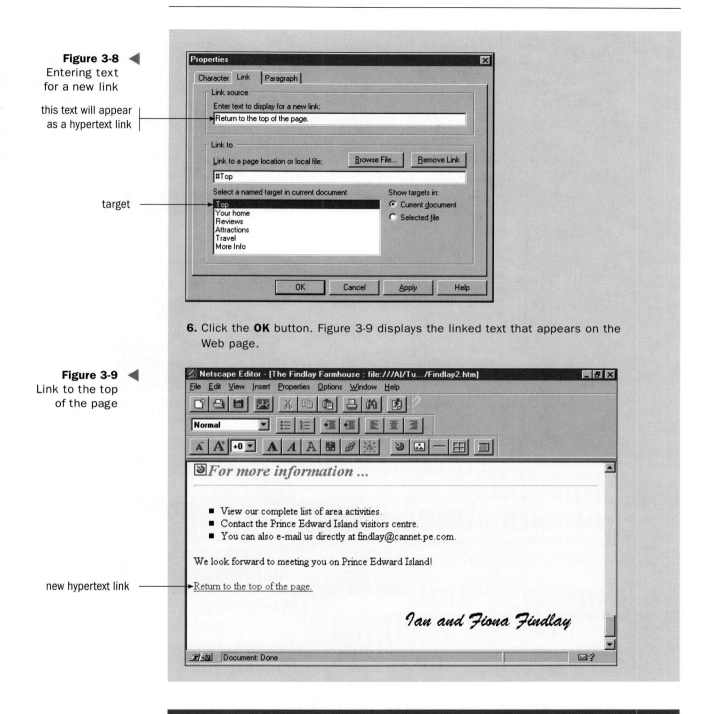

6. Click the **OK** button. Figure 3-9 displays the linked text that appears on the Web page.

Figure 3-9 ◀
Link to the top
of the page

new hypertext link

Testing Links

Once you have entered links into a hypertext document, you should test them in a browser to make sure they jump to the correct targets. You decide to test them in the Netscape browser.

To test the links in the Netscape browser:

1. Click the **View in Browser** button 🖼 on the File/Edit toolbar.

2. Click **Yes** when you are prompted to save your changes to the file. The file appears in the Netscape browser. You can now verify that your hypertext links are working correctly.

3. Move the mouse pointer over the list item, **Your home on Prince Edward Island**. Note that the mouse pointer changes to 🖑 and the status bar shows the name of the file and the drive and folder in which the file is located, followed by a pound sign (#) and the name of the target, Your home. See Figure 3-10.

Figure 3-10 ◀
Testing a link

pointer when you point at a hypertext link

target in status bar

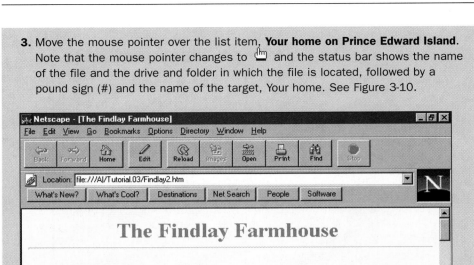

4. Click the **Your home on Prince Edward Island** link. The browser jumps to the Your home target and displays the Your home on Prince Edward Island heading. See Figure 3-11.

Figure 3-11 ◀
Jumping to link's destination

location of Your home target; target icon doesn't appear in browser

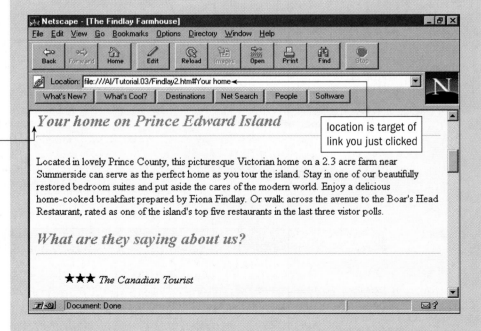

5. Repeat steps 2–4 with the other links on the page to verify that they are all working properly.

> **TROUBLE?** If you discover a link that is not working properly, go back to the Netscape Editor by clicking the Edit button 🖉. Right-click the link in the Netscape Editor, click Link properties, click the Link tab, click the correct target then click the OK button.

You're finished adding hypertext links to the Findlay Web page. Users can now efficiently navigate to different locations on the page. You decide to take a break.

To close all the Netscape windows:

1. Click **File**, then click **Exit**.

2. Click the **Yes** button to close all windows and exit Netscape.

Quick Check

1. What is a target? What is a link?

2. How do you create a target with the Netscape Editor?

3. Are target names case sensitive or case insensitive?

4. How do you convert existing text to hypertext with the Netscape Editor?

5. How do you create new hypertext with the Netscape Editor?

SESSION

3.2

In this session you will create a Web presentation that consists of several documents connected together with hypertext links. You'll learn how to control the development of such multidocument structures through the technique of storyboarding.

Principles of Storyboarding

When you are developing a Web page, one of the first things you must ask yourself is whether you intend to develop and include additional pages on related topics. A structure that contains the primary Web page, additional related pages, and the hypertext links that allow users to move among the pages, is known as a **Web presentation**. Web presentations are usually created by the same person or group, and the pages within a Web presentation usually have the same look and feel.

When you plan your Web presentation, you should determine exactly how you want to relate the pages using hypertext links. Charting the relationship between all the pages in your Web presentation is a technique known as **storyboarding**. Storyboarding your Web pages before you create links helps you determine which structure will work best for the type of information you're presenting and helps you avoid some common problems. You want to make sure readers can navigate easily from page to page without getting lost.

Fiona reminds you that she has developed two other pages for the Findlay Farmhouse Web presentation: Bio, a directory of people on the island, and Events, a list of activities and organizations in the area. Fiona would like readers who access her page to be able to reach either of these pages from the main Findlay Farmhouse page, as shown in Figure 3-12.

Figure 3-12 ◀
Findlay
Farmhouse
Web
presentations

Findlay Farmhouse page

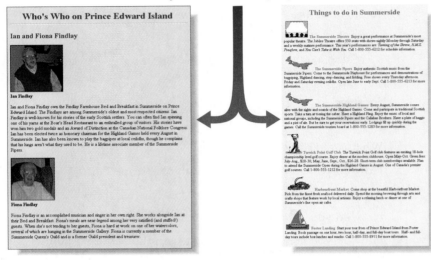

Bio page   Events page

You tell Fiona she should think about the basic principles of structuring Web presentations to decide how to link the three pages together.

Linear Structures

Web presentations can be structured in a number of ways. Examining basic structures can help you decide how to design your Web presentation. Figure 3-13 shows a storyboard for one common structure, the **linear structure**, in which each page is linked to the next and previous pages in an ordered chain of pages.

Figure 3-13 ◀
Linear
structure

in this structure you
can jump only from
one page to the next
or previous page

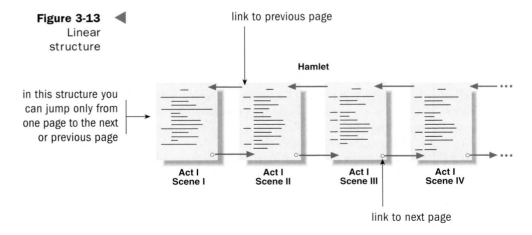

You might use this type of structure in Web pages that have a well-defined order. For example, if you are trying to create a Web presentation of Shakespeare's *Hamlet,* you could create a single Web page for each scene from the play. By using a linear structure, you make it easy for users to progress back and forth through the play. Each hypertext link takes them to either the previous scene or the next scene.

You might, however, want to make it easier for users to return immediately to the opening scene rather than backtrack through several scenes. Figure 3-14 shows how you could include a link in each page that jumps directly back to the first page.

Figure 3-14 ◀
Augmented
linear
structure

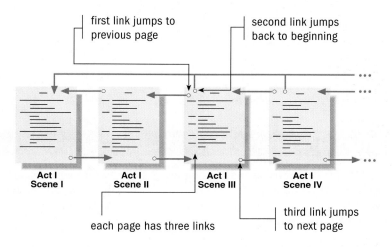

Hierarchical Structures

Another popular structure is the hierarchical structure of Web pages shown in Figure 3-15. A **hierarchical structure** starts with a general topic that includes links to more specific topics. Each specific topic includes links to yet more specialized topics, and so on. In a hierarchical structure, users can move easily from the general to the specific and back again.

Figure 3-15 ◀
Hierarchical
structure

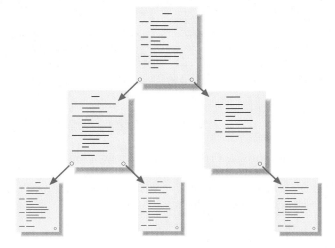

As with the linear structure, including a link to the top of the structure on each page gives users an easy way back to the hierarchy tree. Figure 3-16 shows a storyboard for this kind of Web presentation.

Figure 3-16 ◀
Augmented
hierarchical
structure

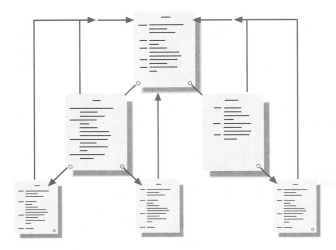

Mixed Structures

You can also combine structures. Figure 3-17 shows a hierarchical structure in which each page level is related in a linear structure. You might use this system for the *Hamlet* Web site to let the user move from scene to scene linearly or from a specific scene to the general act to the overall play.

Figure 3-17 ◀
Combination
of linear and
hierarchical
structures

overall structure
is hierarchical

the scenes

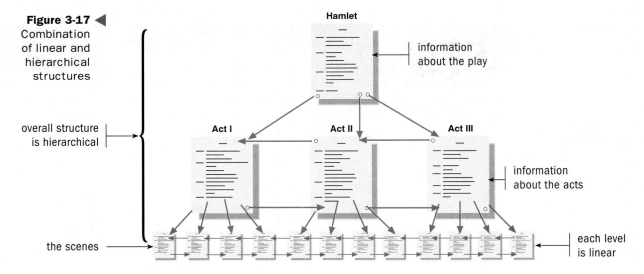

Hamlet

information
about the play

Act I   Act II   Act III

information
about the acts

each level
is linear

As these examples show, a little foresight can go a long way in making your Web pages easier to use. The best time to organize a structure is when you first start creating multiple pages and those pages are small and easy to manage. If you're not careful, you might end up with a structure like the one shown in Figure 3-18.

Figure 3-18 ◀
Web
presentation
with no
coherent
structure

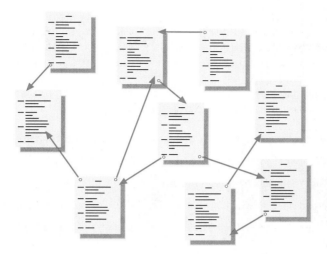

Many of the pages in this Web presentation are isolated from one another, and there is no clear path from one document to another. A user won't know what content to expect when jumping from one link to another. Nor are users ever sure if they have viewed all possible pages.

Creating Links to Other Documents

You and Fiona discuss the type of structure that will work best for the Findlay Farmhouse Web presentation. Fiona wants users to access the Findlay Farmhouse page first, and then both the Bio page and the Events page from the Findlay Farmhouse page. To make navigation easy, she wants hypertext links on both the Bio and Events pages that jump back to the Findlay Farmhouse page. Fiona doesn't see a need to include a hypertext link between the Bio page and the Events page. Based on her recommendations, you draw the storyboard shown in Figure 3-19. Fiona looks it over and agrees that this is what she had in mind.

Figure 3-19 ◀
Structure of
the Findlay
Farmhouse Web
presentation

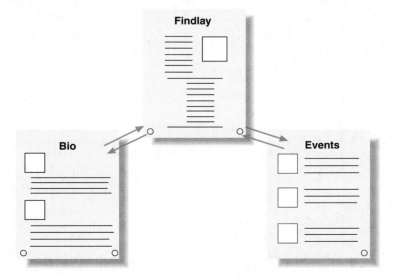

Opening Multiple Documents

Fiona's Web presentation has three pages, and you'd like to be able to work with all of them at once. Unlike some word processors in which you can open several files at one time, the Netscape Editor allows only one open document at a time. However, if you are running Netscape in a multitasking environment like Windows 95, you can run multiple versions of the Netscape Editor simultaneously, with one Web page in each window. The Windows 95 taskbar will then show three Netscape Editor buttons. To identify which button corresponds to which Web page, you point at a button in the taskbar and examine the button name that appears. You need to open Findlay2 (the page you were working on in Session 3.1), Bio, and Events, and then you need to save Bio as Bio2 and Events as Events2, so you don't alter the original files.

To open and rename the files in different Netscape Editor windows:

1. Start Netscape. You do not have to connect to the Internet or load your home page.

2. Click **File**, then click **Open File in Editor**.

3. Locate and open **Findlay2.htm** in the Tutorial.03 folder on your Student Disk.

4. Click **File**, then click **Open File**, then locate and open **Bio.htm** from the Tutorial.03 folder.

5. Click **File**, then click **Save As**.

6. Type **Bio2** in the File name box, then click the **Save** button.

7. Click **File**, then click **Open File**, then locate and open **Events.htm** from the Tutorial.03 folder.

8. Click **File**, then click **Save As**. Type **Events2** in the File name box, then click the **Save** button.

Point at one of the Netscape Editor buttons in the taskbar. Figure 3-20 shows the Events2 page as the active document. If you were to click the button corresponding to the Findlay Farmhouse page, that window would then be the active document.

Figure 3-20 ◀
Opening
multiple Web
documents

name of document

taskbar

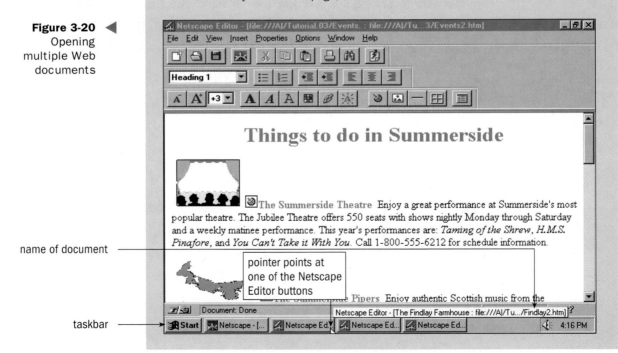

Creating a Hypertext Link Between Two Documents

You create a link between two documents in the same way you created a link to a target within the same document—using the Make Link button 🖉. However, instead of clicking a target, you use the Browse File button to indicate the filename of the page that is the destination of the link.

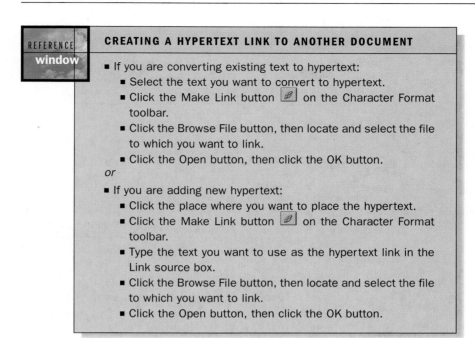

REFERENCE window

CREATING A HYPERTEXT LINK TO ANOTHER DOCUMENT

- If you are converting existing text to hypertext:
  - Select the text you want to convert to hypertext.
  - Click the Make Link button 🖉 on the Character Format toolbar.
  - Click the Browse File button, then locate and select the file to which you want to link.
  - Click the Open button, then click the OK button.

  or

- If you are adding new hypertext:
  - Click the place where you want to place the hypertext.
  - Click the Make Link button 🖉 on the Character Format toolbar.
  - Type the text you want to use as the hypertext link in the Link source box.
  - Click the Browse File button, then locate and select the file to which you want to link.
  - Click the Open button, then click the OK button.

Fiona's three pages are all open in separate Netscape Editor windows. You are ready to create links between the pages. You decide to start by linking the Findlay2 page to the Bio2 page.

To create a hypertext link to the Bio2 page:

1. Click the **Netscape Editor** button on the taskbar that corresponds to the **Findlay2** page.

   TROUBLE? Point at the Netscape Editor buttons on the taskbar until you see one that says Findlay2. Refer back to Figure 3-20 to see this button.

2. Locate the Proprietor information just below the bulleted list at the top of the page.

3. Select the text **Ian and Fiona Findlay**.

4. Click the **Make Link** button 🖉.

5. Click the **Browse File** button.

6. Click **Bio2**, then click the **Open** button. See Figure 3-21.

Figure 3-21 ◀
Creating a link
to another
document

linked text in
document

filename

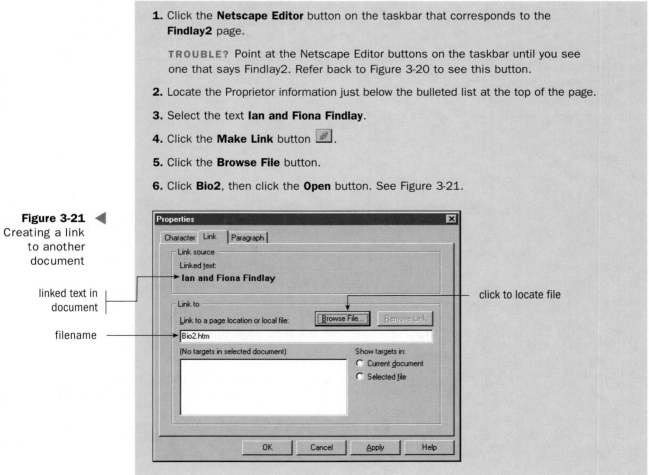

click to locate file

7. Click the **OK** button, then click the Web page to deselect the link.

8. Point to the link and notice the status bar. The Findlay Farmhouse page now displays the text as a hypertext link as shown in Figure 3-22.

Figure 3-22 ◀
Target for this
link is a
different Web
document

link to Bio2 page

name of document

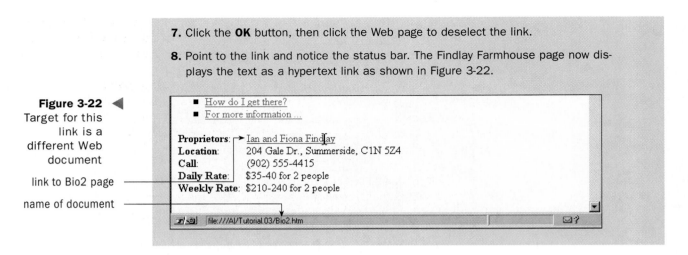

Clicking the link shown in Figure 3-22 will jump you to the Bio2 page. You'll test this link later. Now you are ready to create a hypertext link to the Events2 page.

To create a hypertext link to the Events2 page:

1. Scroll down the document window to the **For more information...** section.

2. Select the text **View our complete list of area activities**.

3. Click the **Make Link** button 🖉.

4. Click the **Browse File** button, click **Events2**, then click the **Open** button.

5. Click the **OK** button, then click the Web page to deselect the link. The text referring to area activities should now be converted to hypertext as is displayed in Figure 3-23.

Figure 3-23 ◀
New hypertext
link

link to Events2 page

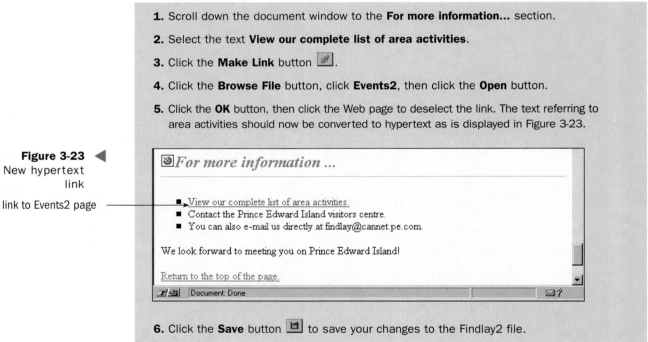

6. Click the **Save** button 🖫 to save your changes to the Findlay2 file.

Now insert links in the Bio2 and Events2 pages that point back to the Findlay2 page. Start with the Bio2 page first.

To create a hypertext link from the Bio2 page to the Findlay2 page:

1. Click the **Netscape Editor** button for the **Bio2** page.

2. Select the text **Findlay Farmhouse Bed and Breakfast** located in the paragraph below the picture of Ian Findlay.

3. Click the **Make Link** button 🖉.

4. Click the **Browse File** button, select the **Findlay2** file, click **Open**, then click the **OK** button.

5. Click the **Save** button 🖫.

Finally, you need to create the hypertext link from the Events2 page back to the Findlay2 page. Since there is no text on the Events2 page that specifically references the Findlays or their bed and breakfast, you will have to insert a hypertext link.

To create a hypertext link from the Events2 page to the Findlay2 page:

1. Click the **Netscape Editor** button for the **Events2** page.

2. Scroll to the bottom of the document window and click to the right of the description of Foster Landing, then press **Enter**.

3. Click the **Make Link** button ⌧.

4. Click the **Browse File** button, select **Findlay2**, then click **Open**.

5. Click the **Enter text to display for a new link** text box.

6. Type **Go to the Findlay Farmhouse page**.

7. Click the **OK** button. Figure 3-24 shows the page with the newly-inserted hypertext link.

Figure 3-24 ◀
Link to Findlay
Farmhouse
page

location of link to
Findlay Farmhouse
page

⌧ Foster Landing Start your tour from of Prince Edward Island from Foster Landing. Book passage on one hour, two hour, half-day, and full-day boat tours. Half- and full-day tours include box lunches and snacks. Call 1-800-555-8911 for more information.

▶ Go to the Findlay Farmhouse page. |

8. Click the **Save** button ⌧.

Testing Your Hypertext Links

Now that the hypertext links are in place, you should return to the Findlay2 page in the browser and then test the links among the three pages to verify that they are working properly.

To test your links:

1. Click the Netscape Editor button for the **Findlay2** page.

2. Click the **View in Browser** button ⌧. The page opens in the Netscape browser.

3. Click the hypertext link **Ian and Fiona Findlay**. The Bio2 page opens in the browser.

4. Scroll down the document window and click the hypertext link, **Findlay Farmhouse Bed and Breakfast**. You return to the Findlay Farmhouse page.

5. Click the **For More Information...** hypertext link to jump down the Findlay Farmhouse page to that heading.

6. Click the hypertext link, **View our complete list of area activities**. The Events2 page is displayed in the browser.

7. Scroll to the bottom of the document window and click the hypertext link, **Go to the Findlay Farmhouse page**. You return to the Findlay Farmhouse page.

8. Click **File**, then click **Close** to close the browser.

Links to Targets Within Other Documents

You can create links not just to other documents, but also to specific points within documents. The destination point must have a target, and the hypertext link you insert must point to that target. You already know how to link to targets within the same document, but now you'll see how to link to targets in a different document.

You and Fiona discuss creating links from the individual items on the Findlay Farmhouse page that correspond to events on the Events2 page. You both agree that it would be a good idea. To save you time, the Events2 page already contains targets for the theatre, bagpiping, golf, and so on. Using those targets, you decide to add links from activities mentioned on the Findlay2 page to the corresponding activity on the Events2 page.

To insert a link to an event on the Events2 page:

1. Be sure the Findlay2 page is active in the Netscape Editor.

2. Scroll to the **Area attractions** section.

3. Select the text **The Summerside Theatre**, then click the **Make Link** button 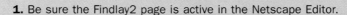.

4. Click the **Browse File** button, click **Events2**, then click **Open**. A list of targets on the Events2 page appears in the target box. See Figure 3-25.

Figure 3-25 ◀
List of targets
in Events2
page

name of page to
which you are linking

list of targets in
Events2 page

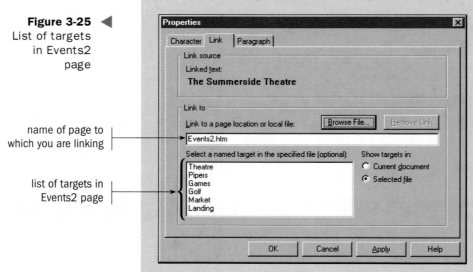

5. Click the **Theatre** target. The target name is appended to the filename, separated by a pound sign (#). See Figure 3-26.

Figure 3-26 ◀
Filename and
target

selected target
appears after the
filename

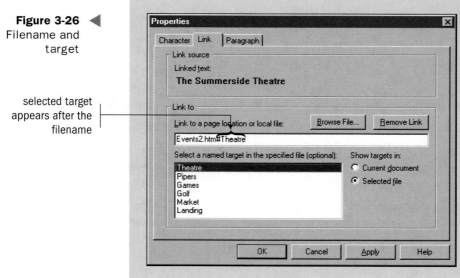

6. Click the **OK** button

7. In a similar manner, link **The Summerside Pipers** to the **Pipers** target and **Turwick Point Golf Club** to the **Golf** target.

8. Save the changes to the Findlay Farmhouse page, then click the **View in Browser** button [image].

9. Scroll to and then test each of the three links and verify that you jump to the appropriate targets in the Events2 page. Click the **Back** button [image] each time you test a link to return to the Findlay Farmhouse page.

TROUBLE? A bug exists in some versions of Netscape Navigator Gold 3.0 that will not accept the target the first time you enter it. If your links do not work, try entering them a second time.

TROUBLE? If a link does not jump to the correct place, open the Findlay2 page in the Netscape Editor, right-click the link, click Link properties, then verify that the correct target is specified. If it isn't, delete it, then repeat the previous set of steps as necessary to correct the link target.

10. Click **File**, then click **Close** to close the browser.

You have now inserted links to the Findlay's Web page that make it easy for users to navigate through the presentation. You decide to take a break.

To close all the Netscape windows:

1. Click any one of the **Netscape Editor** buttons on the taskbar.

2. Click **File**, then click **Exit**.

3. Click the **Yes** button to close all windows and exit Netscape. Click **Yes** again to save your work.

Quick Check

1. What is storyboarding? Why is it important in creating a Web page presentation?

2. What is a linear structure? Draw a diagram of a linear structure and give an example of how to use it.

3. What is a hierarchical structure? Draw a diagram of a hierarchical structure and give an example how to use it.

4. How do you create a hypertext link to another document with the Netscape Editor?

5. How do you create a hypertext link to a target in another document with the Netscape Editor?

SESSION 3.3

In this session you will learn how to create hypertext links to Web pages on the Internet and to Internet resources other than Web pages.

Linking to Web Pages

Up until now you've worked with files all located on the same computer. However, you make use of the real power of the Web when you start linking your document with Web pages on other computers located anywhere from across the hall to across the world. The technique for creating a hypertext link to a Web page on a different computer is very similar to the technique you use to link to documents on your computer, except that instead of specifying the page's filename, you have to specify the page's URL.

As you learned in Tutorial 1, URL stands for Uniform Resource Locator and is the address of a page on the World Wide Web. The URL for a page containing information about majors at MidWest University might be:

http://www.mwu.edu/course/info.html#majors.

URLs can seem complex to new Web users, but they have a very simple and well-defined structure. Figure 3-27 shows the structure of the fictional MidWest University URL about majors.

Figure 3-27 ◀
Parts of
a URL

Part of URL	Interpretation
http	The communications protocol. Web pages use the **HTTP** communications protocol, which stands for **Hypertext Transfer Protocol**. The URL for all Web pages begins with the letters "http". As you'll see later, other Internet resources use different communications protocols. Between the communications protocol and the Internet host name there is a separator, usually a colon followed by a double slash (://).
www.mwu.edu	The Internet host name for the computer storing the Web document.
course	The folder containing the Web document.
info.html	The filename of the Web document.
#majors	The target in the document (optional). The target is preceded by a pound sign (#).

Some Web page URLs, such as http://www.microsoft.com/, do not include the filename section. In cases where the filename is missing, the name of the file is assumed to be index.html.

REFERENCE
window

CREATING A HYPERTEXT LINK TO A DOCUMENT ON THE INTERNET

- If you are converting existing text to hypertext:
  - Select the text you want to convert to hypertext.
  - Click the Make Link button 🖉 on the Character Format toolbar.
  - Enter the URL of the Internet document or resource in the Link to box.
  - Click the OK button.

or

- If you are adding new hypertext:
  - Click where you want to place the hypertext.
  - Click the Make Link button 🖉 on the Character Format toolbar.
  - Type the text you want to use as the hypertext link in the Link source box.
  - Enter the URL of the Internet document or resource in the Link to box.
  - Click the OK button.

Inserting a Hypertext Link to a Web Page

Fiona would like the Findlay Farmhouse page to include a link that points to a Prince Edward Island tourism page. The URL for this page is http://www.gov.pe.ca/vg/start.html. The text for this link is already in place at the bottom of the page.

To insert a link to a page on another computer:

1. Open **Findlay2** from the Tutorial.03 folder in the Netscape Editor.

2. Scroll down to the **For More Information...** section at the bottom of the page.

3. Select the text **Contact the Prince Edward Island visitors centre.**

4. Click the **Make Link** button 🖉.

5. Type **http://www.gov.pe.ca/vg/start.html** in the Link to box as shown in Figure 3-28.

Figure 3-28 ◀
Specifying a
URL as the
link target

URL ——

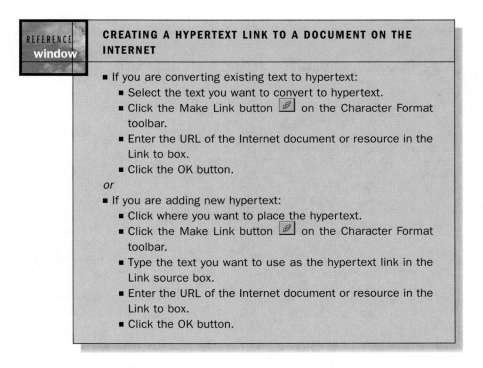

6. Click the **OK** button.

7. Click the **Save** button 🖫 to save the changes to your page.

As usual, you should test your link. To test a link on another computer, you will need to connect to the Internet.

To test this hypertext link:

1. Connect to the Internet and make sure the **Findlay2** page is the active page in the browser.

2. Return to the Netscape Editor.

3. Click the **View in Browser** button 🖾.

4. Click the **Contact the Prince Edward Island visitors centre** hypertext link. The tourism page appears as shown in Figure 3-29.

TROUBLE? If the page does not appear, it could be because you are not connected to the Internet or that the Web server that is storing this page is not working. If the page looks different from the one shown in the figure, it could be because the page has changed since the time this tutorial was written.

Figure 3-29 ◀
Prince Edward
Island Visitors
Guide on
the Web

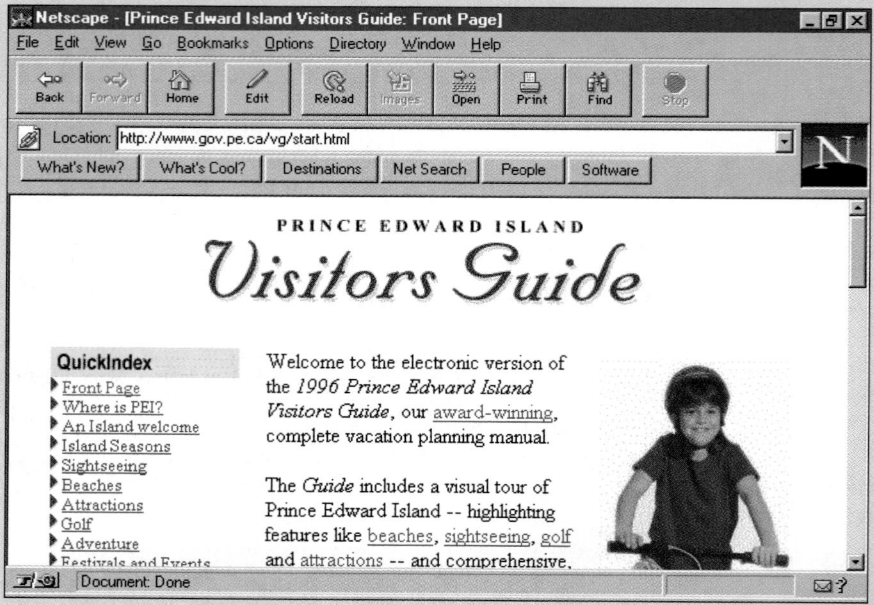

Creating a Link Using Drag and Drop

The Netscape Editor offers an even easier way to add links to your Web page. The **drag and drop** technique involves dragging a hypertext link from the Netscape browser window and dropping it into the Netscape Editor window. This useful technique helps you avoid typing errors, because you don't have to type long and complicated URLs. The Findlays would like a link to a page featuring places to go sightseeing on the island besides those around Summerside. The tourism page that you just accessed includes a page with such information. You can drag the link to that page directly into your document.

To create a link through dragging and dropping:

1. Resize the browser and Netscape Editor windows so that you can see both on your desktop.

2. Click within the **Netscape Editor** window to make it the active window.

3. Add a new list item in the Editor window by clicking the end of the item, "Contact the Prince Edward Island visitors centre" at the bottom of the page and pressing **Enter**. See Figure 3-30.

Netscape
Browser
window

Figure 3-30
Positioning the
Editor and
Browser
windows

Netscape Editor
window

you'll drop link here

you'll drag this link

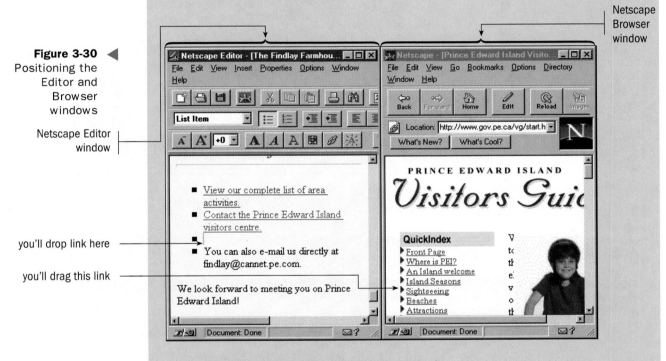

4. Click the **Netscape browser** window to activate it.

5. Point to the **Sightseeing** link on the Tourism page with the Browser window, and, with the mouse button held down, drag the pointer across to the Netscape Editor window as shown in Figure 3- 31.

TROUBLE? If you click the Sightseeing link by mistake, click the Back button , then repeat step 5.

Figure 3-31 ◄
Inserting a link
using drag
and drop

pointer changes when
you are dropping
a link

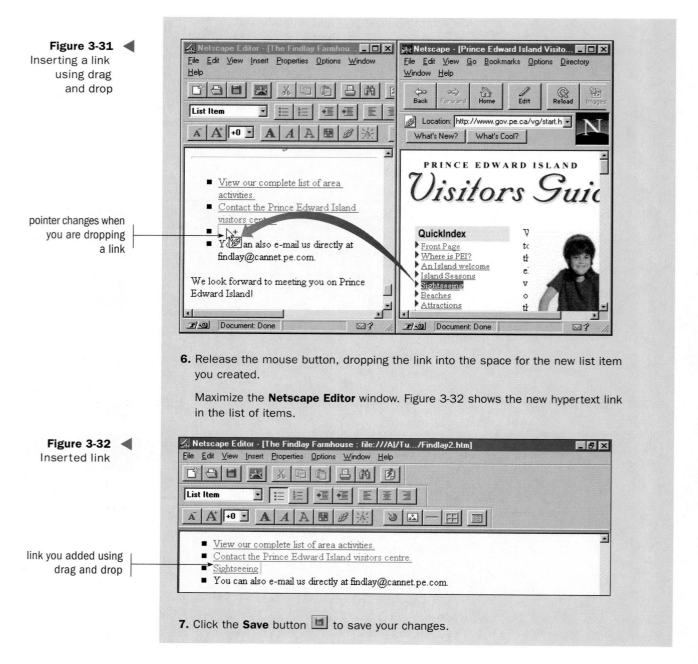

6. Release the mouse button, dropping the link into the space for the new list item you created.

Maximize the **Netscape Editor** window. Figure 3-32 shows the new hypertext link in the list of items.

Figure 3-32 ◄
Inserted link

link you added using
drag and drop

7. Click the **Save** button 🖫 to save your changes.

As usual, you should confirm that the link you just created works.

To check your new hypertext link:

1. Click the **View in Browser** button ⊞. Scroll to the bottom of the page, then click the **Sightseeing** link.The Sightseeing page appears as shown in Figure 3-33.

Figure 3-33 ◀
Target of link
you dragged
and dropped

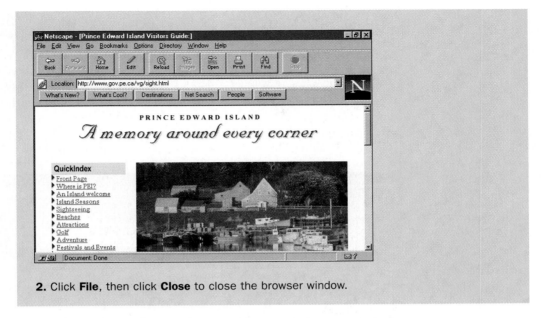

Figure 3-33 ◀
Target of link
you dragged
and dropped

2. Click **File**, then click **Close** to close the browser window.

Linking to Other Internet Resources

You can link to other Internet resources besides Web pages. These include FTP servers, Usenet newsgroups, Gopher servers, and e-mail addresses. Creating a link to one of these resources requires that you enter the proper URL. Each of these resources employs a different communications protocol in its URL. For example, Web pages use the HTTP protocol, but FTP servers use the FTP protocol, as you'll see.

Linking to FTP Servers

FTP servers store files that users on the Internet can download or transfer to their computers. **FTP** stands for File Transfer Protocol and is the communications protocol used by these file servers to transfer information. URLs for FTP servers follow the same format as for Web pages, except they use the FTP protocol rather than the HTTP protocol. The general form of the URL is ftp://*Hostname*, where *Hostname* is the Internet host name of the FTP server. For example, to create a link to the FTP server located at ftp.microsoft.com, you should use the URL ftp://ftp.microsoft.com in the hypertext link. Figure 3-34 shows this particular FTP server as it appears in the Netscape browser.

Figure 3-34 ◀
FTP server at
ftp.microsoft.
com

URL for FTP server ─

files and folders on
the FTP server

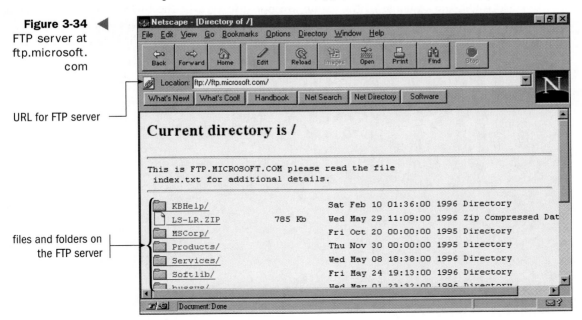

Linking to Gopher servers

Before the World Wide Web, **Gopher servers** were popular tools that organized the resources of the Internet through the use of hierarchical menus, from which you selected the Internet resource you wanted. While Gopher has become a less popular tool as use of the Web grows, you might still need to access a Gopher server. The form of the URL for a Gopher server is gopher://*Hostname*, where *Hostname* is the Internet host name of the Gopher server. For example, the URL for a Gopher server at gopher.wisc.edu is gopher://gopher.wisc.edu. Figure 3-35 shows this particular Gopher server as it appears in the Netscape browser.

Figure 3-35 ◀
Gopher
server at
gopher.wisc.edu

URL for Gopher server ——

Gopher menu as it
appears in the
document window

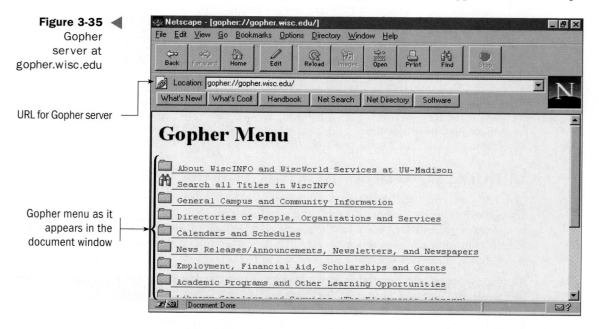

Linking to Usenet Newsgroups

Usenet is a collection of discussion forums, called **newsgroups**, to which users can send and retrieve messages on a wide variety of topics. The form of the URL for a particular news-group is: news:*newsgroup* where *newsgroup* is the name of the forum. For example, the URL for the newsgroup alt.surfing is news:alt.surfing. When you access a newsgroup with Netscape, the contents of the group are not displayed in the browser window. Instead, Netscape starts a special program called a **newsgroup reader** that gives you access to all the messages in the group. Accessing the alt.surfing newsgroup opens the news reader window shown in Figure 3-36.

Figure 3-36
Accessing the
alt.surfing
newsgroup

alt.surfing
newsgroup

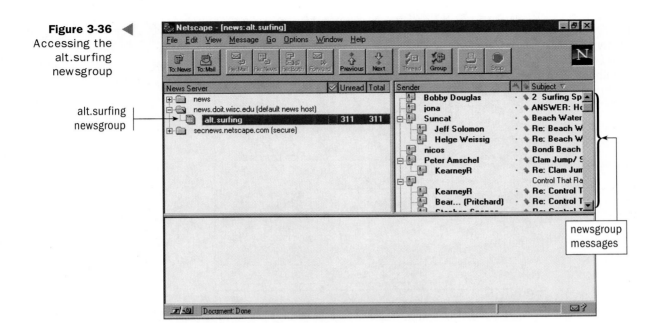

newsgroup
messages

Not all Web browsers can work with the newsgroup URL, so you might want to be cautious in including links to newsgroups in the Web documents you create.

Linking to E-mail Addresses

Many Web authors include their e-mail address on their Web pages so that they can receive direct feedback from people who use the page. The URL for an e-mail address is: mailto: *e-mail_address* where *e-mail_address* is the Internet e-mail address of the user. For example, if a user's e-mail address is davis@mwu.edu, the URL for this address is mailto:davis.mwu.edu. When someone reading the page clicks this e-mail address link, Netscape starts its built-in e-mail program from which the user can create and send an e-mail message. As with newsgroups, not all browsers can work with the e-mail hypertext link.

In order to make it easy for people to contact them, the Findlays have included their e-mail address on their Web page. You suggest that they make this a hypertext link.

To create a link to an e-mail address:

1. Return to the **Findlay2 Netscape Editor** window.

2. Scroll to the bottom of the page and select the text **findlay@cannet.pe.com** from the For more information... section.

3. Click the **Make Link** button.

4. Type **mailto:findlay@cannet.pe.com** in the Link to box as shown in Figure 3-37.

Figure 3-37 ◀
Creating an
e-mail link

e-mail link ──────→

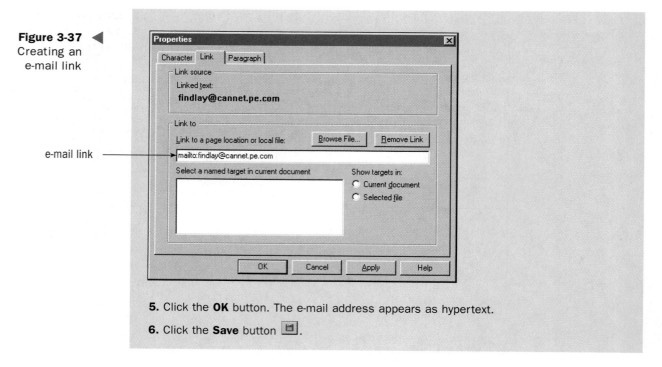

5. Click the **OK** button. The e-mail address appears as hypertext.

6. Click the **Save** button 🖫 .

Now you should test this link to verify that it works properly.

To test your e-mail address link:

1. Click the **View in Browser** button 🖳 .

2. Scroll to the bottom of the page and click **findlay@cannet.pe.com**.

3. Netscape starts its e-mail program, automatically placing the address in the Mail
to field as shown in Figure 3-38. At this point you could type a message and
send it off. For now, you should simply exit without sending anything (the e-mail
address is fictional).

   TROUBLE? If a message appears telling you that you don't have a return e-mail
   address, click the OK button, then skip step 3.

Figure 3-38 ◀
Netscape's
e-mail program

4. Click **File**, then click **Close**.

The Findlay Farmhouse home page is now complete. Ian and Fiona are very pleased with its final appearance. They decide to work with it for a few days and let you know if they need any more help. For now you can close Netscape and take a break.

To close all the Netscape windows:

1. Click **File**, then click **Exit**.

2. Click the **Yes** button to close Netscape.

Quick Check

1. What are the five parts of a URL?

2. What is the URL for a file named info.htm located in the /flowers/inventory folder of the Web server whose host name is www.ftd.com?

3. What is the URL for the FTP server located at ftp.umich.edu?

4. What is the URL for the newsgroup rec.sports.basketball.pro?

5. What is the URL for the e-mail address baker@csw.edu?

Tutorial Assignments

Ian and Fiona have had a chance to work with the page you created. They would like you to make the following changes:

- Add a link to the Events2 page that takes the user from the bottom of the page to the top.

- On the Events2 page, include a note that Ian Findlay is honorary chairman of the Highland Games. Include a link to the Bio2 page.

- Include a link on the Events2 page that points to the official Prince Edward Island list of events and attractions located at http://www.gov.pe.ca/vg/attract.html.

To complete this tutorial assignment:
1. Open the Events2.htm file in the Netscape Editor.
2. Insert a target named "Top" at the beginning of the main heading.
3. Scroll to the bottom of the page and add a new line, "Return to the top of the page."
4. Link the text to the target named "Top" that you just created.
5. Scroll up to the description of the Highland Games. Add the following text to the end of the paragraph:
   "You can also contact Ian Findlay, this year's honorary chairman, care of the Findlay Farmhouse Bed and Breakfast."
6. Select the text "Ian Findlay" from the sentence you just entered and link it to the Bio2 page in the Tutorial.03 folder.
7. Scroll down to the bottom of page and add a new line:
   "For more events and attractions, go to the Prince Edward Island list of current attractions".
   Note: Make sure you do not make the line you add a continuation of the existing link when you press Enter. If your new line does continue the link, highlight the new line, then choose Remove Links from the Edit menu.
8. Select the text "Prince Edward Island list of current attractions" and link it to the URL http://www.gov.pe.ca/vg/attract.html.
9. Save your changes to the "Events3.htm" file.
10. Open the Events3 page in the browser to confirm that the links are working properly.
11. Print the page.
12. Hand in the printout to your instructor.

Case Problems

1. The Author Series at Avalon Books Avalon Books is adding a new set of pages to their home page that will include biographical information for authors making appearances at the bookstore. They've asked you to set up the hypertext links between the bookstore's home page and the biographical pages.

To complete this case problem:

1. Start the Netscape Editor and open the file "Avalon3.htm," located in the Cases folder in the Tutorial.03 folder on your Student Disk.
2. Save the file as "Avalon4" in the Cases folder.
3. Scroll down to the list of the coming week's events.
4. Select the text "Sandy Davis" and create a hypertext link to the file "SD.htm," located in the Cases folder in the Tutorial.03 folder on your Student Disk.
5. Select the text "John Sheridan" and create a hypertext link to the file "JS.htm" in the Cases folder in the Tutorial.03 folder on your Student Disk.
6. Save your changes to the Avalon4 file.
7. Open the file in the Netscape browser and confirm that the links are working correctly.
8. Print the Avalon4 page.
9. Hand in the printout to your instructor.

2. Creating a List of Movie Reviewers You want to create a Web page for the Film School that lists pages containing reviews and synopses of major movies. You've received a list of existing pages and their URLs from your instructor. See Figure 3-39. Create a Web page of this list. Format the list as a bulleted list with a solid square bullet. Make each page name a hypertext link to the appropriate Web page. Add the title "Movie Review Pages" at the top of the Web page.

Figure 3-39 ◀

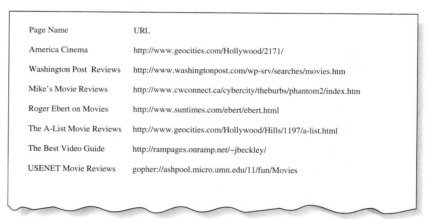

Page Name	URL
America Cinema	http://www.geocities.com/Hollywood/2171/
Washington Post Reviews	http://www.washingtonpost.com/wp-srv/searches/movies.htm
Mike's Movie Reviews	http://www.cwconnect.ca/cybercity/theburbs/phantom2/index.htm
Roger Ebert on Movies	http://www.suntimes.com/ebert/ebert.html
The A-List Movie Reviews	http://www.geocities.com/Hollywood/Hills/1197/a-list.html
The Best Video Guide	http://rampages.onramp.net/~jbeckley/
USENET Movie Reviews	gopher://ashpool.micro.umn.edu/11/fun/Movies

To complete this case problem:

1. Open a blank document in the Netscape Editor.
2. In the Document Properties dialog box, on the General tab, type "Movie Review Pages" in the Title box.
3. Type your name in the Author box, and type "A list of useful movie review Web pages" in the Description text box.
4. Save the page as "Movie.htm" in the Cases folder on your Student Disk.
5. Type the main heading "Movie Review Pages," formatted with the Heading 1 style and centered on the page.
6. Create a bulleted list of the page names shown in Figure 3-39.
7. Select the bulleted list and using the Properties dialog box, choose the solid square symbol for the bullets.

8. Select each item in the list and link the entire text in the item to the URL specified in Figure 3-39.
9. Save your changes to the file.
10. View the file in the Netscape browser and confirm that each link is working correctly.
11. Create a printout of your Web page.
12. Hand in the printout to your instructor.

3. Personnel Pages at First City Bank The systems manager at First City Bank is creating Web pages listing company employees and their positions. Figure 3-40 shows one such page that details the bank's loan officers. Each photo on the page is linked to another page that gives more detail about the employee. The three employee pages are located on your Student Disk in the Cases folder in the Tutorial.03 folder with the filenames Keller.htm, Flint.htm, and Taylor.htm. Create the page shown in Figure 3-40, including the hypertext links to these three files.

Figure 3-40 ◄

First City Bank

Loan Officers

Loan Officer, Linda Keller

Loan Officer, Laura Flint

Assistant Loan Officer, Mary Taylor

To complete this case problem:
1. Open a blank document in the Netscape Editor.
2. In the Document Properties dialog box on the General tab, type "First City Bank Loan Officers" in the Title box.
3. Type your name in the Author box, then type "Loan officers at First City Bank" in the Description box.
4. Save the page as "Bank.htm" in the Cases folder in the Tutorial.03 folder on your Student Disk.

5. Type the main heading "First City Bank," formatted with the Heading 1 style and centered on the page.

6. Insert a horizontal line after the main heading that covers the width of the page.

7. Type the title "Loan Officers," formatted with the Heading 2 style and left-aligned on the page.

8. Insert the graphic image file "Keller.gif" on the first line below the Loan Officers heading.

9. Type "Loan Officer, Linda Keller" to the right of her photo.

10. Insert the graphic image file "Flint.gif" on the next line.

11. Type "Loan Officer, Laura Flint" to the right of her photo.

12. Insert the graphic image file "Taylor.gif" on the next line.

13. Type "Assistant Loan Officer, Mary Taylor" to the right of her photo.

14. Select each of the three photos, and using the Make Link button, link the photos to the files Keller.htm, Flint.htm, and Taylor.htm.

15. Save your changes to the file.

16. Open the "Bank.htm" file in the Netscape browser and verify that the links are working properly.

17. Print a copy of your page.

18. Hand in your printout to your instructor.

4. Create your own Web presentation Create a Web presentation about yourself. There should be three pages in the presentation. The first page should deal with your interests. Include an ordered list of your top-ten favorite Web pages. The second page should deal with your coursework. Include a bulleted list detailing your previous courses. The third page should be a resume page that you could submit to an employer. Include short summaries of your work experience and educational background. Create hypertext links between the three pages including links to specific points within each page using targets. The appearance of the page is up to you. Use whatever colors, page backgrounds, or inline images that you think are appropriate.

Using Tables in Your Web Pages

Creating a Products Table

OBJECTIVES

In this tutorial you will:

- Create a text table using fixed-width fonts, nonbreaking spaces, and line breaks

- Learn how to use the Formatted paragraph style

- Create a graphical table

- Format text in a graphical table

- Modify the appearance of a graphical table

- Add and remove rows and columns from a graphical table

- Create table cells that span more than one row or column

- Insert inline images into a graphical table

CASE

Middle Age Arts

Middle Age Arts is a company that creates and sells replicas of historic European works of art for home and garden use. They specialize in sculpture, tapestries, prints, friezes, and busts. One of their biggest sellers is the Gargoyle Collection, which consists of replicas of gargoyles from famous cathedrals around the world. Nicole Garibaldi, the head of advertising at Middle Age Arts, is directing the effort to place the products catalog on the World Wide Web. She wants the page to contain each product's name, its item number, price, and the type and finish of the piece. Nicole has asked you to create the Web pages for the Gargoyle Collection. She'd like you to start by creating a prototype page using just a few products. Figure 4-1 shows you what she has in mind.

Figure 4-1 ◀
Nicole's
products table

Name	Item#	Type	Finish	Price
Bacchus	48059	Wall Mount	Interior Plaster	$95
Praying Gargoyle	48159	Garden Figure	Gothic Stone	$225
Spitting Gargoyle	48184	Garden Figure	Gothic Stone	$200
Gargoyle Judge	48222	Bust	Interior Plaster	$275

To display this information on the Gargoyle Collection Web page, you'll need to create a **table**, a grid with rows and columns. The table will display each product in its own row, and the features of the products will be displayed in the columns.

SESSION

4.1

In this session you will use the Netscape Editor to create a simple text table. To format the table properly, you'll learn to create non-breaking spaces and line breaks. You will also learn about proportional and fixed-width fonts and the effects of each in creating text tables for your Web pages. Finally, you will be introduced to the Formatted paragraph style, which simplifies the process of creating a text table.

Tables on the World Wide Web

There are two ways to insert a table into a Web page. You can create a **text table** like the one shown in Figure 4-2, in which text is evenly spaced out on the page into rows and columns. Text tables use only standard typewriter characters, so even a line in a text table is created by repeating a typographical character, such as a hyphen, underline, or equal sign, as you can see in Figure 4-2.

Figure 4-2 ◀
Example of
a text table

```
                     Computer Models


Manufacturer             Model              Price
------------------------------------------------
City Computers           P325 Plus          $2500
Midwest CPU              586/Ultra          $2700
CowCity Computers        P133/+             $2450
CMF Computers            P150z              $2610
```

all text table elements
are created using
typewriter characters

You can also create a **graphical table**, as shown in Figure 4-3, where the table appears as a graphical element on the Web page.

Figure 4-3
Example of a
graphical table

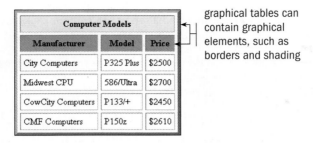

graphical tables can
contain graphical
elements, such as
borders and shading

Graphical tables are more flexible than text tables and can be more attractive, but there is one drawback to using a graphical table. Not all browsers, such as the text-based Lynx browser used on many UNIX systems, can display graphical tables. For this reason, many Web authors create two versions of their Web pages: one that uses only text elements and text tables and another that takes advantage of graphical elements. You advise Nicole that for this reason you should prepare two versions of the Gargoyle Collection page: one with a text table and one with a graphic table. She agrees, and you decide to create the text table first.

Creating a Text Table

You create a text table by inserting characters and spaces that define the column widths. Figure 4-4 shows the spaces required to create a two-column text table. You must manually enter the spaces between each column.

Figure 4-4
Spacing in a
text table

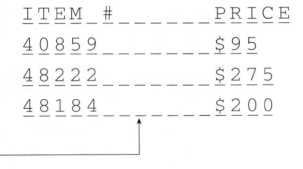

you must enter
correct number of
spaces in each row
to align second
column correctly

To save you typing, the page header and introductory paragraph of your Middle Age Arts page has already been created and saved in a file. You'll open this file and then save it with a new name so you don't alter the original file.

To open the Arts file and then save it with a new name:

1. Double-click the **Netscape Navigator** icon 🔲 on your computer's desktop or within the Netscape program window.

2. If your computer tries to initiate an Internet connection, click the **Cancel** button. You do not need to be connected to the Internet.

3. Click the **Stop** button 🔲 if your browser attempts to load your home page.

4. Click **File**, then click **Open File in Editor**.

5. Locate and select the file **Arts** from the Tutorial.04 folder on your Student Disk. Figure 4-5 shows the page.

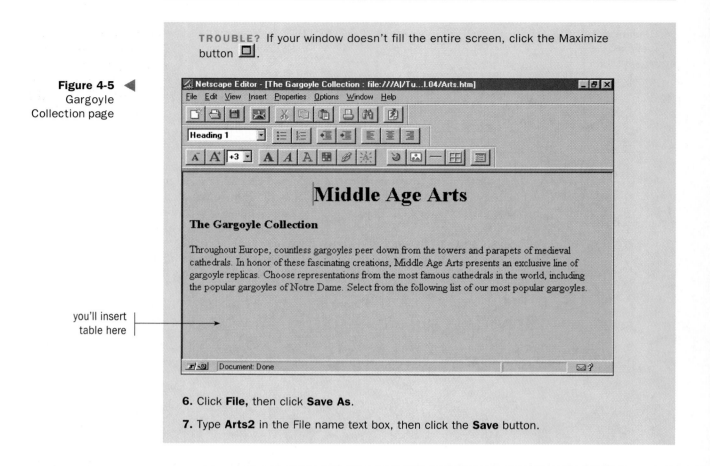

Figure 4-5 ◄
Gargoyle
Collection page

you'll insert
table here

6. Click **File**, then click **Save As**.

7. Type **Arts2** in the File name text box, then click the **Save** button.

Using Fixed-width Fonts

Because a text table relies on spaces and the characters that fill those spaces to create its column boundaries, you have to make sure you use a font that takes up the same amount of space per character. Netscape allows you to specify two types of fonts in your Web pages: proportional fonts and fixed-width fonts.

   In a **proportional font** the width of each individual character differs depending upon the form of the character. For example, the letter "m" requires more space than the letter "l." In contrast, **fixed-width fonts** use the same amount of space for each character regardless of the character's form. Figure 4-6 shows the difference between the two fonts. Notice that a proportional "m" is much wider than its fixed-width counterpart, whereas a proportional "l" is much narrower than its fixed-width counterpart.

Figure 4-6 ◄
Proportional
vs. fixed-width
font

proportional font
allots different
width to each
letter, depending
on letter width

fixed-width font
allots same width
to each letter

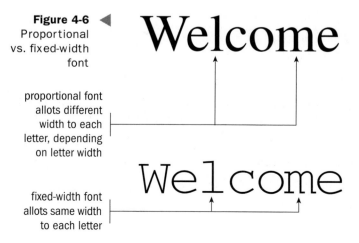

Most typeset documents (such as the one you're reading now) use proportional fonts, but in creating a text table it is important that you use fixed-width fonts. If you used a proportional font in a text table, the varying width of the characters might cause errors in the table formatting. For example, Figure 4-7 shows how a text table that uses a proportional font loses alignment when the font size is increased or decreased. Because the browser determines the size of the font in the text, you should not use a proportional font if you want the text table to look right to all users.

Figure 4-7 ◀
Column
alignment
problems with
proportional
font

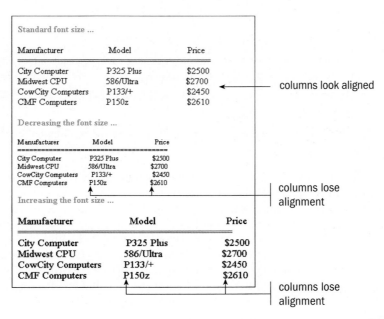

By contrast, the table shown in Figure 4-8 uses fixed-width fonts. Note that the columns remain aligned regardless of font size.

Figure 4-8 ◀
Column
alignment with
fixed-width font

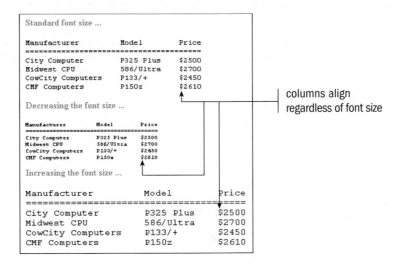

You decide to start creating the table with a fixed-width font. Refer back to Figure 4-1 to remind yourself of the information you are going to enter. You'll start by entering the heading row.

To start creating the text table of products:

1. Click the end of the opening paragraph, then press **Enter**.

2. Click the **Fixed Width** button A .

3. Type **Name** for the first heading in the table.

Before you enter the next heading, Item #, you need to understand how to enter the spaces that will align the second column.

Entering Nonbreaking Spaces and Line Breaks

If you were typing columns on a typewriter, you would move from one column to the next either by pressing the Spacebar several times or by pressing the Tab key. Neither of these methods work with the Netscape Editor. Try it!

To try moving to the next column of the table:

1. Press **Spacebar** several times. Netscape inserts a single space, but refuses to insert additional spaces—no matter how many times you press Spacebar.

2. Press **Tab**. Netscape *indents* the entire line rather than tabbing over. Something is wrong.

3. Click the **Decrease Indent** button to remove the indent.

What went wrong? Recall that the formatting on your page is accomplished through HTML tags. In working with the Netscape Editor, you might forget that the tags are there, but the Editor doesn't. Placing additional spaces between your text characters is considered formatting and thus can be accomplished only through a tag or special symbol. Similarly, tabs are also not recognized by HTML. The Netscape Editor uses the tab as a keyboard shortcut to increase indenting. So how do you place a row of spaces in your line? You use **nonbreaking spaces**—spaces between words that will allow for multiple spaces. To insert a nonbreaking space into your document you hold down the Shift key as you're pressing the Spacebar. Nonbreaking spaces can be used with proportional as well as fixed-width fonts.

Try inserting nonbreaking spaces into the Gargoyle Collection text table.

To insert a set of nonbreaking spaces between columns and enter the remaining table headings:

1. Hold down the **Shift** key and press **Spacebar** fourteen times to create a total of fifteen spaces between the first and second column (remember you already added one space).

2. Type **Item #**.

3. Hold down the **Shift** key and press **Spacebar** five times.

4. Type **Type**.

5. Hold down the **Shift** key and press **Spacebar** fifteen times.

6. Type **Finish**.

7. Hold down the **Shift** key and press **Spacebar** fifteen times.

8. Type **Price**. Figure 4-9 shows the complete table heading row.

Figure 4-9 ◀
Table heading
row

table heading row ⎯⎯⎯⎯

The Gargoyle Collection

Throughout Europe, countless gargoyles peer down from the towers and parapets of medieval cathedrals. In honor of these fascinating creations, Middle Age Arts presents an exclusive line of gargoyle replicas. Choose representations from the most famous cathedrals in the world, including the popular gargoyles of Notre Dame. Select from the following list of our most popular gargoyles.

Name	Item #	Type	Finish	Price

Document: Done

Creating a Text Table Line

To help separate the heading row from the data in a text table, you can add a dividing line. Since this is a text table, you should create the line using a text symbol such as the equal sign character (=) rather than a graphical horizontal line so that the line appears on text-based browsers. The line looks best if it appears directly under the table's heading row. As you might have noticed, pressing the Enter key at the end of a line causes the Netscape Editor to start a new paragraph, inserting additional space between the end of the old paragraph and the start of the new. This is not what you want—you want the divider to be close to the heading row. You can get around this problem by inserting a line break. A **line break** tells the browser to display text on the next line *within the same paragraph*. You create line breaks by holding down the Shift key as you press the Enter key. In the steps, holding two keys at the same time is shown with the + symbol, such as Shift + Enter.

REFERENCE window | **INSERTING NONBREAKING SPACES AND LINE BREAKS**
- To insert a nonbreaking space, press Shift + Spacebar.
- To insert a line break, press Shift + Enter.

To add a dividing line to your text table:

1. Hold down the **Shift** key on your keyboard and press the **Enter** key.

2. Press and hold down the **=** key to create a line of ='s under the column heading until you reach the end of the line. Figure 4-10 displays the appearance of the line in the Document window.

Figure 4-10 ◀
Dividing line
created of
equal sign
characters

dividing line ———

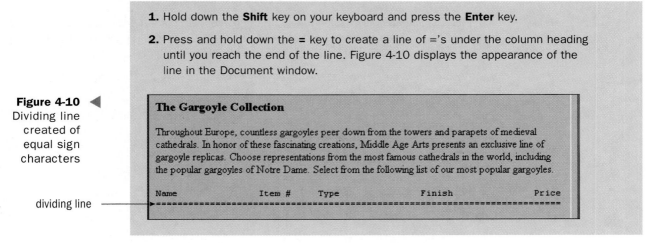

The Gargoyle Collection

Throughout Europe, countless gargoyles peer down from the towers and parapets of medieval cathedrals. In honor of these fascinating creations, Middle Age Arts presents an exclusive line of gargoyle replicas. Choose representations from the most famous cathedrals in the world, including the popular gargoyles of Notre Dame. Select from the following list of our most popular gargoyles.

Name	Item #	Type	Finish	Price

Using the Formatted Style

So far you have entered text by manually specifying a fixed-width font and nonbreaking spaces. You can use one of the paragraph styles, the Formatted paragraph style, to accomplish the same thing. The Formatted paragraph style formats the text as a fixed-width font and interprets *all* spaces as nonbreaking spaces.

You decide to use the Formatted paragraph style to finish the text table for Middle Age

REFERENCE window

CREATING A TEXT TABLE
■ Click the Fixed Width button.
■ Type the contents of the table, inserting line breaks and non-breaking spaces where appropriate.
■ Press Shift + Spacebar to create nonbreaking spaces and Shift + Enter to insert a line break.
or
■ Click the Formatted paragraph style.
■ Type the contents of the table.
■ Press Spacebar to insert spaces and Shift + Enter to insert line breaks.

Arts's Gargoyle Collection page.

To finish the table using the Formatted paragraph style:

1. Press **Shift + Enter**.

2. Click the **Paragraph style** list arrow ▼ on the Paragraph Format toolbar.

3. Click **Formatted**.

4. Type **Bacchus**.

5. Press **Spacebar** twelve times to line up the cursor with the left edge of the second column, then type **48059**. Note that with the Formatted paragraph style you do not have to press the Shift key as you press Spacebar.

6. Use the Spacebar to move to the left edge of the third column, then type **Wall Mount**.

7. Move to the Finish column, then type **Interior Plaster**.

8. Move to the Price column, then type **$95**.

9. Press **Shift** + **Enter** to go to a new line in the table.

10. Finish inserting the following table entries, copied from Figure 4-1:

Praying Gargoyle	**48159**	**Garden Figure**	**Gothic Stone**	**$225**
Spitting Gargoyle	**48184**	**Garden Figure**	**Gothic Stone**	**$200**
Gargoyle Judge	**48222**	**Bust**	**Interior Plaster**	**$275**

Remember to press Shift + Enter at the end of each line. The completed table should appear as shown in Figure 4-11.

Figure 4-11 ◀
Completed text
table

text table ⟶

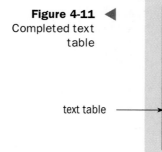

As you've seen, there are several key combinations that are helpful to keep in mind as you create text tables. Figure 4-12 summarizes some of the common key combinations you can use with the Netscape Editor.

Figure 4-12 ◀
Text table key
functions

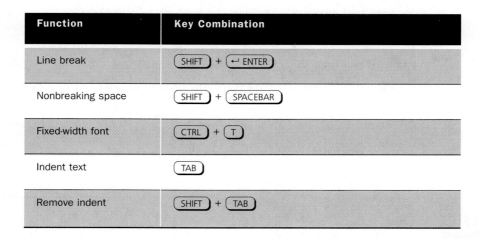

Function	Key Combination
Line break	SHIFT + ↵ ENTER
Nonbreaking space	SHIFT + SPACEBAR
Fixed-width font	CTRL + T
Indent text	TAB
Remove indent	SHIFT + TAB

The table is finished. Save your work and view the completed page in the Netscape browser.

To save your changes and view the file in the browser:

1. Click the **Save** button 🖫.

2. Click the **View in Browser** button 🖾. Figure 4-13 shows the completed page.

Figure 4-13 ◀
Gargoyle
Collection page
in browser

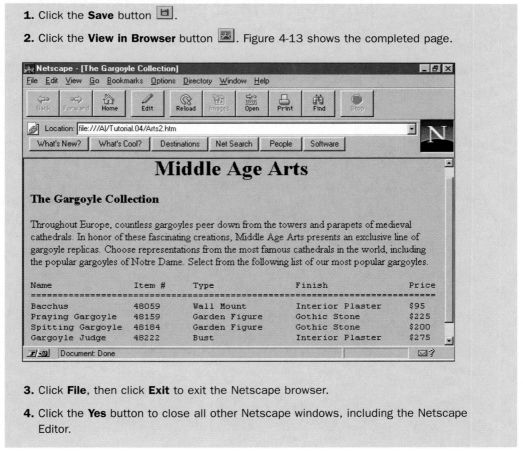

3. Click **File**, then click **Exit** to exit the Netscape browser.

4. Click the **Yes** button to close all other Netscape windows, including the Netscape Editor.

You show the completed page to Nicole. She's very pleased with your work and is anxious for you to create a similar page using a graphical table. You'll start working on that page in the next session.

Quick Check

1. What is a text table? What is a graphic table? Why would you use a text table rather than a graphic table on a Web page?

2. What are fixed-width and proportional fonts?

3. What can happen to a text table if you create it using a proportional font?

4. What are nonbreaking spaces? How do you insert a nonbreaking space with the Netscape Editor?

5. What are line breaks? How do you insert line breaks with the Netscape Editor?

6. What is the Formatted paragraph style?

SESSION 4.2

In this session you'll create a graphical table. You'll learn how to format text within the table and how to modify the table's appearance.

Working with the Netscape Editor Table Tool

Now that you have completed the first prototype page for Nicole, you are ready to start working on the second. The first page was designed for people who use text-based browsers. Now you need to create a page for users with graphical browsers that can display graphical tables. To create this table, you'll use the Netscape Editor Table tool, which creates a graphical grid of rows and columns. The intersection of each row and column is called a **cell**. When you first create a graphical table, the width of the cell is determined by the text you enter into the cell.

Unlike inline images, you cannot wrap text around a graphical table. Instead the table occupies a single line by itself. You can, however, specify whether the table is aligned with the left or right edge of the screen or is centered.

As with the previous prototype page, the Web document has already been created for you. Since this page is intended to be viewed by people who have graphical browsers, it includes elements that the previous page did not, such as the Middle Age Arts logo and a background pattern.

To open the Arts3 file and save it with a new name:

1. Start Netscape.

2. If your computer tries to initiate an Internet connection, click the **Cancel** button. You do not need to be connected to the Internet.

3. Click the **Stop** button 🔲 if your browser attempts to load your home page.

4. Click **File**, then click **Open File in Editor**.

5. Locate and open **Arts3** from the Tutorial.04 folder on your Student Disk. Figure 4-14 shows the page.

Figure 4-14 ◀
Gargoyle
Collection page
in browser

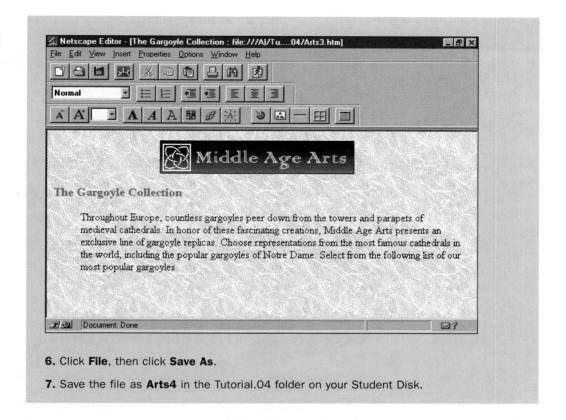

6. Click **File**, then click **Save As**.

7. Save the file as **Arts4** in the Tutorial.04 folder on your Student Disk.

Creating a Table

You create a table using the Insert Table button ⊞ on the Character Format toolbar. This button opens a dialog box that lets you specify the number of rows and columns you want in your table.

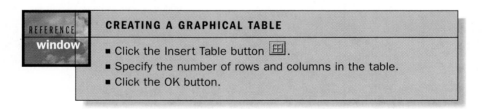

REFERENCE
window

CREATING A GRAPHICAL TABLE

- Click the Insert Table button ⊞.
- Specify the number of rows and columns in the table.
- Click the OK button.

The products table you'll be inserting needs five rows and five columns, called a 5×5 table. Thus you'll be able to enter data into twenty-five cells.

To insert a graphic table on the Arts4 page:

1. Click the end of the introductory paragraph.

2. Click the **Insert Table** button ⊞ on the Character Format toolbar.

3. Type **5** in the Number of rows box, then press **Tab**.

4. Type **5** in the Number of columns box. Figure 4-15 shows the completed Create Table dialog box.

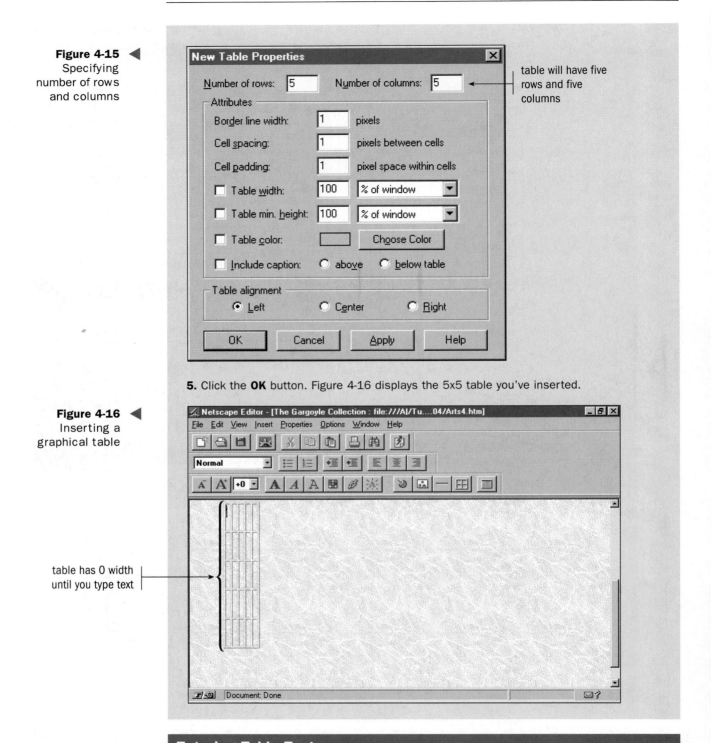

Figure 4-15 ◀
Specifying
number of rows
and columns

table will have five
rows and five
columns

5. Click the **OK** button. Figure 4-16 displays the 5x5 table you've inserted.

Figure 4-16 ◀
Inserting a
graphical table

table has 0 width
until you type text

Entering Table Text

The width of the table is determined by the text entered into the table cells. In Figure 4-16, there is no text in the table cells, so the cells have a width of zero. To enter text in a cell, you click it and then type the text. As you enter the text into a cell, the width of the cells in that column increases to accommodate the text.

When adding text to your table, you move from cell to cell by pressing the Right Arrow key (→) on your keyboard. You cannot move between cells by pressing the Tab key. Recall that the Tab key is a keyboard shortcut that the Netscape Editor uses to insert an indent. To move from the end of one row to the beginning of the next, you also press →, rather than pressing the Enter key, which inserts an extra line into the current table cell. You'll start entering table text with the table headings.

To add headings to your table:

1. If necessary, click the cell in the first row and column of the table.

2. Type **Name** then press → on your keyboard. Note that as you type the column heading, "Name," the column expands to the width of the text.

   TROUBLE? If you accidentally press the Tab key, click the Decrease Indent button ⊞ on the Paragraph Format toolbar.

3. Type **Item #** then press →.

4. Type **Type** then press →.

5. Type **Finish** then press →.

6. Type **Price** then press → to move to the next row in the table. Figure 4-17 shows the first row of the table.

Figure 4-17 ◀
Table heading
row

row you just entered ——————

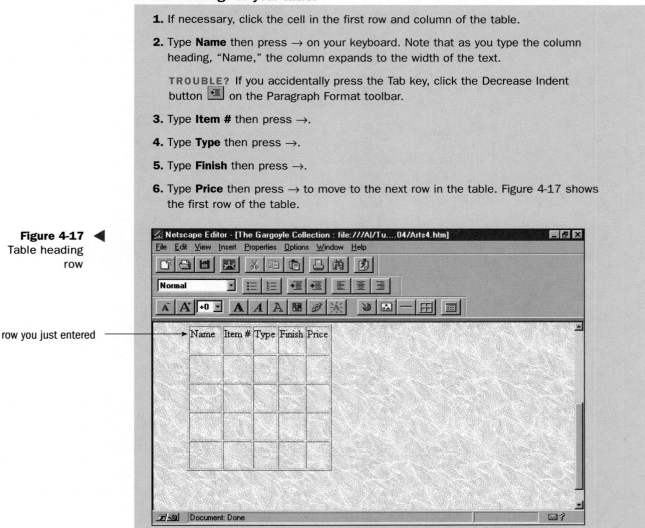

With the headings in place, you can enter the remaining rows of product information.

To enter the remaining product information:

1. Type **Bacchus** then press →.

2. Type **48059** then press →.

3. Type **Wall Mount** then press →.

4. Type **Interior Plaster** then press →.

5. Type **$95** then press → to go to the next row of the table.

6. Finish inserting the following table entries, copied from Figure 4- 1:

Praying Gargoyle	**48159**	**Garden Figure**	**Gothic Stone**	**$225**
Spitting Gargoyle	**48184**	**Garden Figure**	**Gothic Stone**	**$200**
Gargoyle Judge	**48222**	**Bust**	**Interior Plaster**	**$275**

Figure 4-18 shows the completed table.

Figure 4-18 ◀
Completed
table

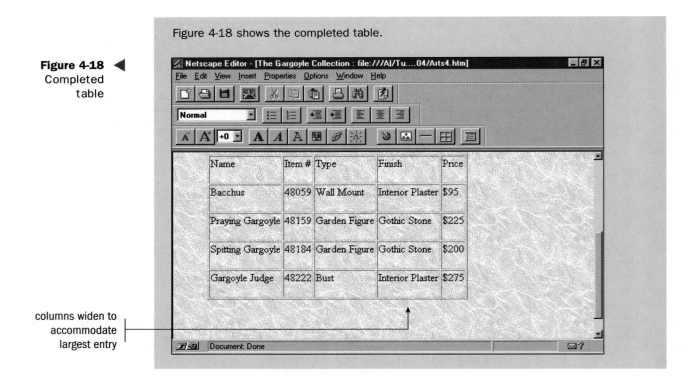

columns widen to
accommodate
largest entry

The Netscape Editor does not always display the table exactly as it will appear in the browser. There are some differences in how the space between the text in a cell and the cell border appear. To check your table's appearance in the browser, save the file and view it with the page with the Netscape browser.

To view the Arts4 page in the browser:

1. Click the **Save** button ▨.

2. Click the **View in Browser** button ▨ then scroll down to view the table. Figure 4-19 shows the page as it appears in the Netscape browser. Note that the borders around the text in each cell have less space than was indicated in Figure 4-18 from the Netscape Editor.

WORKING WITH THE NETSCAPE EDITOR TABLE TOOL   **NG 131**

Figure 4-19 ◀
Table as it
appears in
browser

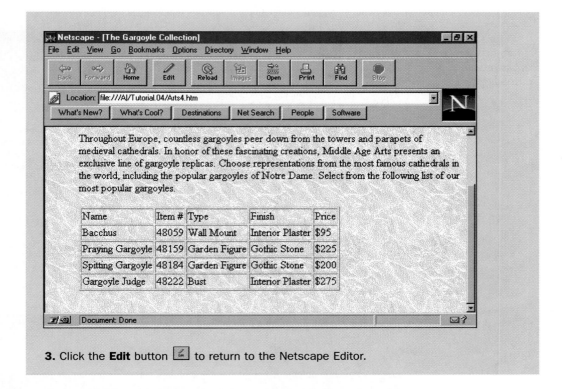

3. Click the **Edit** button to return to the Netscape Editor.

Creating Table Headings

Tables usually include either a row or column that contains headings for the table. For example, in your table, the first row contains titles for each of the five table columns. Cells that contain headings for table rows or columns are called **table headers**. The Netscape Editor allows you to define a cell as a table header. Specifying a cell as a table header causes the text within the cell to be boldfaced and centered, allowing it to stand out from the rest of the text in the table.

To create table headers:

1. Click the first cell in the table.

2. Click the **Object Properties** button.

3. Click the **Cell** tab.

4. Click the **Header style** check box to select it.

5. Click the **OK** button to close the dialog box. The first cell containing the "Name" heading is now boldfaced and centered.

6. Repeat steps 1-5 to change the property of each remaining cell in the first row to the Header style.

TROUBLE? The Netscape Editor does not allow you to select all cells in a row at the same time. You must change the property for each cell individually. Figure 4-20 shows the formatted table headers.

Figure 4-20 ◀
Table headers
formatted with
Header style

table headers
now formatted

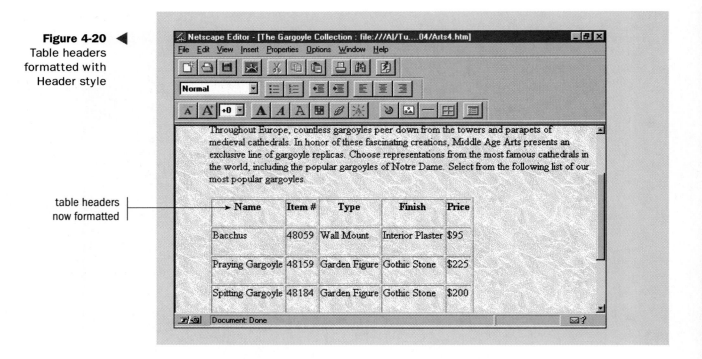

Adding a Table Caption

You can also add a **caption** to your table, a line located at either the top or bottom of the table that describes the table's contents. The Netscape Editor centers captions above or below the table. They "travel" along with the table if you decide to move the table to a new location on the Web page. You decide to add a caption below the products table that you just created.

To add a table caption:

1. Click any cell within the table.
2. Click the **Object Properties** button 🔲.
3. Click the **Table** tab.
4. Click the **Include caption** check box, then click the **below table** option button.
5. Click the **OK** button.
6. Click a point directly below the table.
7. Type **Order your gargoyle today!** Figure 4-21 shows the table and caption.

Figure 4-21 ◀
Adding a
table caption

table caption

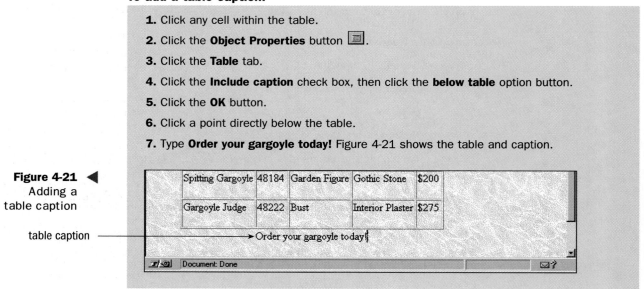

Aligning Text Within a Cell

As you are working on the table, Nicole drops by to see how things are coming along. She notices that the price figures in the fifth column are not properly lined up. She suggests you align them so they are easier to read. Text within each cell of the table can be left-, center-, or right-aligned. By default, text is left-aligned when first entered. You decide to right-align the values in the Price column.

To right-align the price values:

1. Click the cell containing the price value for the wall mount of Bacchus in the second row of the table.

2. Click the **Object Properties** button 🔳.

3. Click the **Cell** tab.

4. Click the **Right** option button within the column of Horizontal text alignment options.

5. Click the **OK** button.

6. Repeat steps 1-5 with the remaining Price cells, except for the header. Figure 4-22 displays the revised table.

Figure 4-22 ◀
Right-aligning
cells

prices are
right-aligned

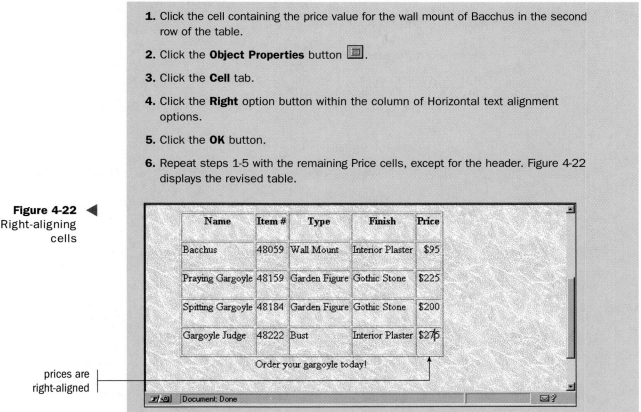

Working with the Appearance of Your Table

Until now you've worked only with the appearance of text within your table. You now want to modify the appearance of the table itself. This includes specifying the size of the table, the width and height of each table cell, the size of the cell borders, and the color of the table background.

The Netscape Editor allows you to change the properties for specific cells within the table, for an entire row or for the entire table. However, you cannot change the properties for an entire column at once. Some properties, such as cell width, affect all cells within a column, but others require you to modify each cell in the column separately. You've already had to do something like this when you modified the text alignment in the Price column.

Specifying the Table Size

In the products table you've created, the size of the table is determined by the text you placed in it. As you entered additional text, the size of the table and the cells increased as necessary. This resulted in a table whose cell borders closely hugged the text. Tight borders might make the text look constricted. You can avoid this problem by making the table larger, giving the text more room within each cell.

The Netscape Editor offers two ways to resize a table. You either specify the size as a percentage of the width and height of the document window or you express the width and height in number of pixels. Expressing the width in terms of the document window ensures that your table is sized relative to the size of the display area. The pixel option ensures that your table has a fixed width and height regardless of the size of the display area. If you use this option, you don't want a table width greater than 640 pixels or a table height of greater than 480 pixels, because many monitors are set to a standard dimension of 640x480 pixels and will not be able to display the entire table within the document window.

You decide that you would like to set the table size to 550 pixels in width, but you'll leave the table height settings alone.

To set a width for your table:

1. Click anywhere within the borders of the table.

2. Click the **Object Properties** button 🔲.

3. Click the **Table** tab.

4. Click the **Table width** check box, then type **550** in the corresponding box.

5. Click the **Width** list arrow then click **Pixels**. Figure 4-23 displays the completed Table dialog box.

Figure 4-23 ◄
Setting a new
table width

table width settings —————

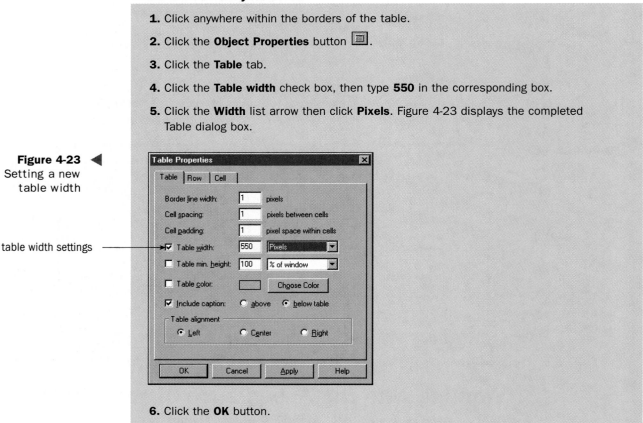

6. Click the **OK** button.

Increasing the size of the table increases the size of each column or row proportionally. Thus the Finish column, which was originally much wider than the Price column, is increased by a correspondingly greater amount when you widen the table. Since the Netscape Editor does not perfectly preview the appearance of the table, you decide to view the change to the table in the Netscape browser.

To view your page in the Netscape browser:

1. Click the **Save** button 🔲.

2. Click the **View in Browser** button 🔲. Figure 4-24 shows the current table—here the Finish column looks fine.

Figure 4-24 ◀
Viewing the
resized table in
the browser

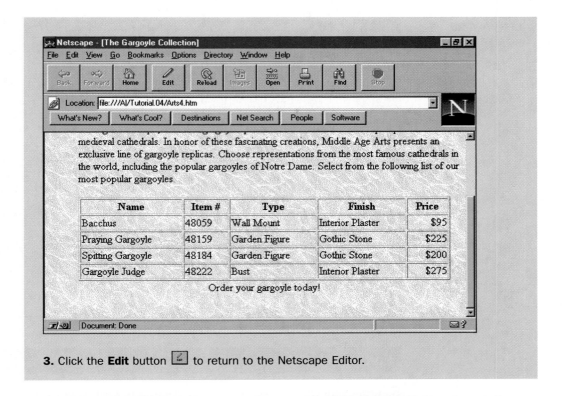

medieval cathedrals. In honor of these fascinating creations, Middle Age Arts presents an exclusive line of gargoyle replicas. Choose representations from the most famous cathedrals in the world, including the popular gargoyles of Notre Dame. Select from the following list of our most popular gargoyles.

Name	Item #	Type	Finish	Price
Bacchus	48059	Wall Mount	Interior Plaster	$95
Praying Gargoyle	48159	Garden Figure	Gothic Stone	$225
Spitting Gargoyle	48184	Garden Figure	Gothic Stone	$200
Gargoyle Judge	48222	Bust	Interior Plaster	$275

Order your gargoyle today!

3. Click the **Edit** button to return to the Netscape Editor.

Changing the Width of a Single Column

You have several options in setting your column width. You can specify the width of a single cell within the colum. This will guarantee that the width of the column will be no less than the width specified for that cell, but it might still expand to encompass any text that you enter. If you want to make sure the column will be set to a certain width and will not expand, you have to specify that width for every cell in the column. Nicole reminds you that when you create the final version of the Gargoyle Collection, you'll be adding new gargoyle types that will require more space to describe. After trying several different widths for the Type column, you decide that 175 pixels will be sufficient. Since you want the columns always to be 175 pixels wide, you will set the width for every cell in the column.

To change the width of the Type column:

1. Click the cell containing the "Type" header.

2. Click the **Object Properties** button .

3. Click the **Cell** tab.

4. Click the **Cell Width** check box, type **175** in the corresponding box, click the **Width** list arrow, then click **Pixels**.

5. Click the **OK** button. Figure 4-25 shows the expanded Type column.

6. Proceed to change the widths of the other cells in the Type column.

Figure 4-25 ◀
Enlarged Type
column

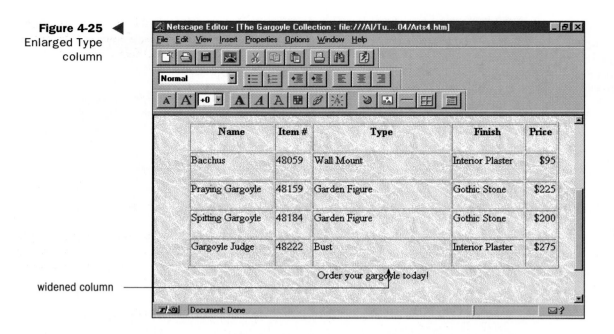

widened column ───

Editing the Table Border, Cell Spacing, and Cell Padding

Besides changing the size of the table itself, a row or a cell, you can also change the size of certain table elements. Figure 4-26 identifies three of these elements: the table border, the spacing between table cells, and the padding within cells.

Figure 4-26 ◀
Samples of
table elements

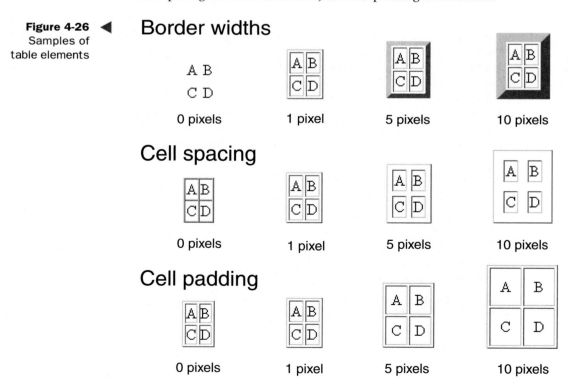

The **table border** is the outside boundary of the table. As you can see from Figure 4-26, increasing the size of the border width gives your tables more of a 3-D look. The default table border width is 1 pixel. If you want to remove the lines from your table entirely, you can set the table border width to 0 pixels.

Cell spacing is the space between the cells in the table. Figure 4-26 displays the effect of increasing the spacing between cells. The default cell spacing is 1 pixel.

Finally, **cell padding** is the space between the cell text and the cell boundary. You might want to increase the default cell padding value, which is one pixel, if you feel the text is too cramped within the cell borders. Figure 4-27 shows a table that features a customized border width, cell spacing, and cell padding.

Figure 4-27 ◀

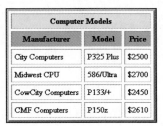

You decide to change the values of the table border, cell spacing, and cell padding to enhance your table's appearance. You would like to increase the table border width to ten pixels in order to give the table the illusion of depth. You decide to reduce the cell spacing to 0 pixels and increase the cell padding to 3 pixels.

To change values for the table border, cell spacing, and cell padding:

1. Click anywhere within the products table.

2. Click the **Object Properties** button 🔲.

3. Click the **Table** tab.

4. Type **10** in the Border line width box, then press **Tab**.

5. Type **0** in the Cell spacing box, then press **Tab**.

6. Type **3** in the Cell padding box. Figure 4-28 shows the completed dialog box.

Figure 4-28 ◀
Changing table
elements

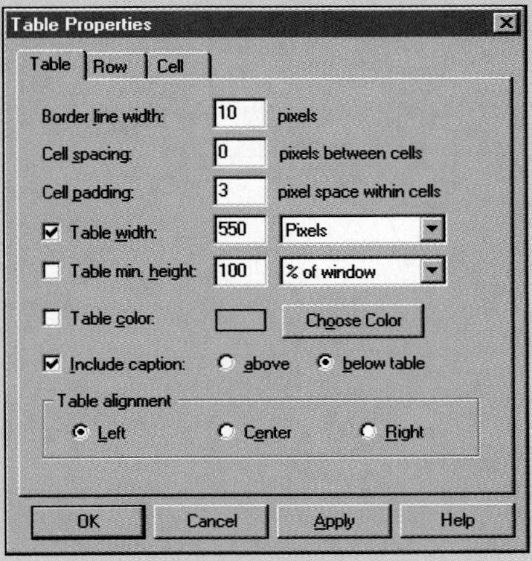

7. Click the **OK** button. Figure 4-29 shows the table's new appearance.

Figure 4-29 ◀
Table with
new design

revised table
elements

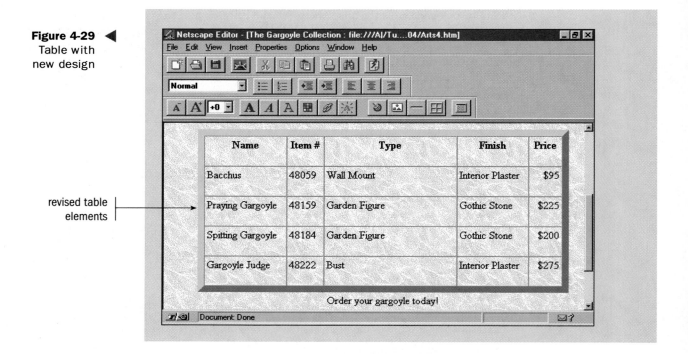

Defining Table Colors

The Netscape Editor also allows you to add colors to the cells in your table. You can add colors to all the cells in the table, all cells in a single row, or to a single cell. Nicole would like the information about each reproduction placed on a solid white background and the table headers placed on a yellow background.

To add color to your table:

1. Click a cell in the first row of the table (the one containing the table headers), then click the **Object Properties** button 🖾.

2. Click the **Table** tab.

3. Click the **Choose Color** button.

4. Click the white square from the color palette (the entry in the sixth row and eighth column), then click the **OK** button.

5. Click the **Row** tab.

6. Click the **Choose Color** button.

7. Click the yellow square from the color palette (the entry in the first row and second column), then click the **OK** button.

8. Click the **OK** button to close the Table Properties dialog box. Figure 4-30 shows your table with colors.

Figure 4-30 ◀
Changing a
table's colors

table headers
are yellow

background is white

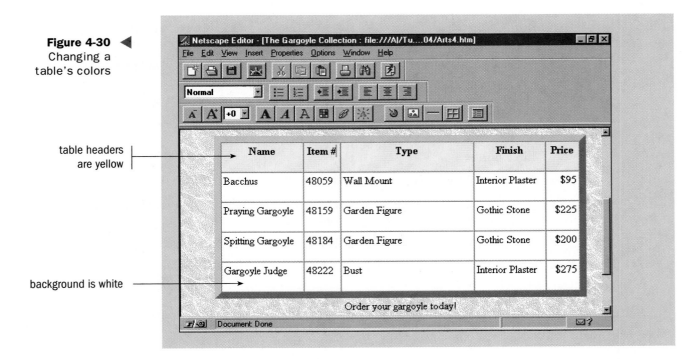

You decide to take a break from working on the table. You'll show Nicole your progress and get her feedback.

To view the current state of your page and exit Netscape:

1. Click the **Save** button 🖫, then click the **View in Browser** button 📷.Figure 4-31 shows the page as it appears in the browser.

Figure 4-31 ◀
Table as it
appears in
the browser

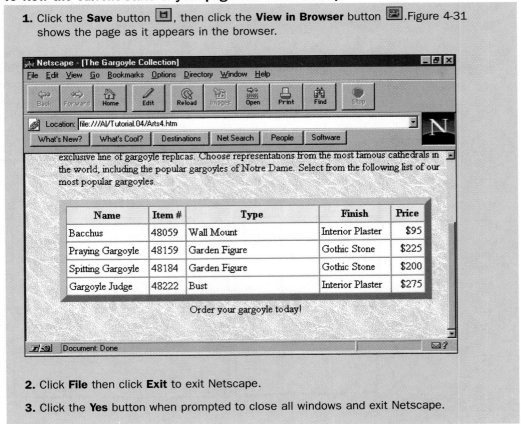

2. Click **File** then click **Exit** to exit Netscape.

3. Click the **Yes** button when prompted to close all windows and exit Netscape.

Quick Check

1. What are table headers and how do you create them with the Netscape Editor?

2. Define the following terms:

   Cell spacing

   Cell padding

   Table border

3. Describe the two ways of specifying table size.

4. How would you create a table that covers the entire document window for all users no matter what their monitor resolution?

5. How would you create a column that is exactly 250 pixels wide?

6. How would you create a column that is at least 250 pixels wide?

SESSION 4.3

In this session you'll further modify the appearance of your table by adding and removing rows and columns. You'll also learn how to create a cell that spans several rows and columns. Finally, you'll learn how to wrap text within a single cell and to insert images in your tables.

Modifying the Table Structure

Nicole has had a chance to review your table. She would like to suggest a few changes. She wants to remove the Type and Finish columns and replace them with a single column called "Description," which would include a descriptive sentence or paragraph about each item. She also wants you to add another item to the table: the Gargoyle Judge model, created for outdoor use such as in a garden. Finally she wants to include a photograph of each product in the table. Figure 4-32 shows the type of table that she has in mind.

Figure 4-32 ◀
Nicole's suggestions for Gargoyle Collection table

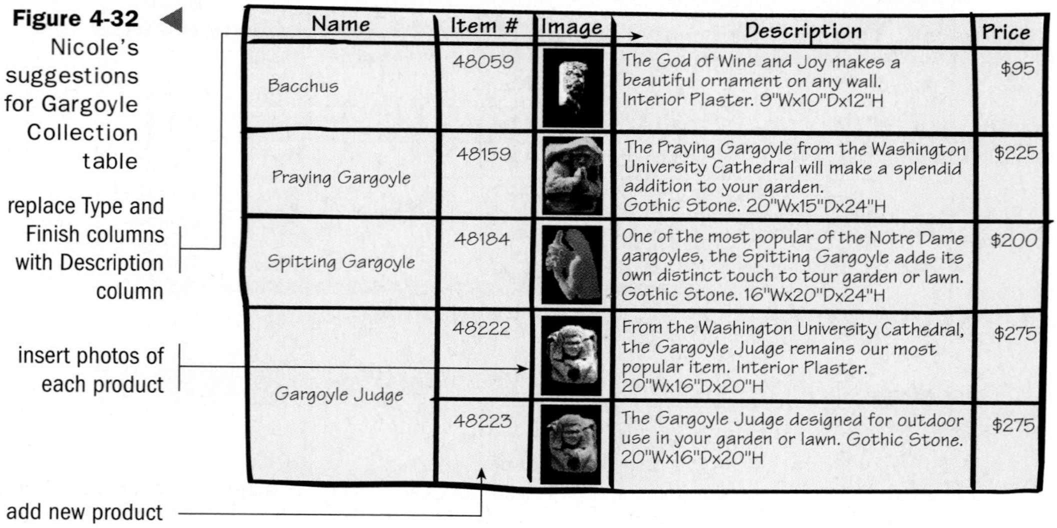

replace Type and Finish columns with Description column

insert photos of each product

add new product

Name	Item #	Image	Description	Price
Bacchus	48059		The God of Wine and Joy makes a beautiful ornament on any wall. Interior Plaster. 9"Wx10"Dx12"H	$95
Praying Gargoyle	48159		The Praying Gargoyle from the Washington University Cathedral will make a splendid addition to your garden. Gothic Stone. 20"Wx15"Dx24"H	$225
Spitting Gargoyle	48184		One of the most popular of the Notre Dame gargoyles, the Spitting Gargoyle adds its own distinct touch to tour garden or lawn. Gothic Stone. 16"Wx20"Dx24"H	$200
Gargoyle Judge	48222		From the Washington University Cathedral, the Gargoyle Judge remains our most popular item. Interior Plaster. 20"Wx16"Dx20"H	$275
	48223		The Gargoyle Judge designed for outdoor use in your garden or lawn. Gothic Stone. 20"Wx16"Dx20"H	$275

To begin, open the Arts4 file you created in the last session and save it as Arts5 so you don't alter the original.

To open the Arts4 page:

1. Start Netscape, then open the **Arts4** file located in the Tutorial.04 folder on your Student Disk, in the Netscape Editor.

2. Click **File** then click **Save As**, type **Arts5** in the File name text box, then click the **Save** button.

Removing and Inserting Rows and Columns

To revise the table according to Nicole's suggestions, you'll need to remove and then add some columns and rows. To remove columns or rows from a table you must select a cell from the column or row that you want to remove. You then use the Delete Table command on the Edit menu. A submenu opens that allows you to delete the column or row containing the selected cell, or the entire table.

You need to remove the Type and Finish columns.

To remove the Type and Finish columns:

1. Click one of the cells in the Type column.

2. Click **Edit**, point to **Delete Table,** then click **Column**. The Type column is removed.

   TROUBLE? If you choose the wrong table element from the Delete Table sub-menu, you can undo the deletion by choosing the Undo option from the Edit menu.

3. Click one of the cells in the Finish column.

4. Click **Edit**, point to **Delete Table,** then click **Column**. The Finish column is removed. Figure 4-33 shows the table.

Figure 4-33 ◀
Table with Type and Finish columns deleted

columns widen because table is set to fixed width

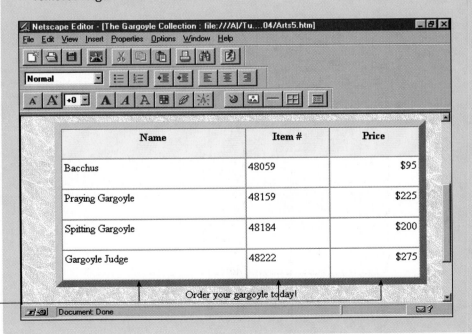

As you deleted each column, the size of the remaining columns increased. This is because you fixed the width of the table in the last session at 550 pixels. The table will remain this size no matter how many columns you add or remove.

You are now ready to add two new columns—the Image column and the Description column.

To insert new columns into the table:

1. Click any cell in the Item # column.

2. Click **Insert**, point to **Table**, then click **Column**.

3. Click **Insert**, point to **Table**, then click **Column** again.

The two new columns are added to the table between the Item # and Price columns. You decide to fix the width of the first new column at 50 pixels and the second new column at 300 pixels.

To fix the width of the two new columns:

1. Click the cell in the first row and third column of the table.

2. Click the **Object Properties** button ⊞.

3. Click the **Cell** tab.

4. Click the **Cell width** check box, type **50** in the corresponding box, click the **Cell width** list arrow, then click **Pixels**.

5. Click the **OK** button.

6. Repeat this process for the remaining cells in the column.

7. Click the cell in the first row and fourth column, then click the **Object Properties** button ⊞.

8. Click the **Cell width** check box, type **300**, click the **Cell width** list arrow, then click **Pixels**.

9. Click the **OK** button.

10. Repeat this process for the remaining cells in the column.

Finally you have to add a new row to the table for the gargoyle that Nicole wants you to add.

To insert a new row in the table:

1. Click a cell in the last row of the table.

2. Click **Insert**, point to **Table**, then click **Row**. A new row is added to the table. Figure 4-34 shows the structure of the table with the new columns and the new row added.

Figure 4-34 ◀
Table with
added columns
and row

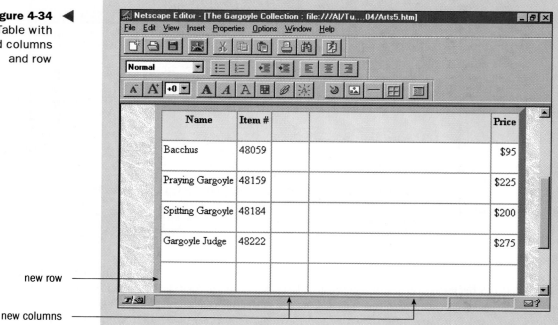

new row

new columns

Spanning a Cell Across Rows and Columns

The final modification you have to make to structure the table like Nicole's sketch in Figure 4-32 is to create a spanning cell. A **spanning cell** is a single cell that covers more than a single row and/or column. Figure 4-35 shows a table of opinion poll data that includes several spanning cells. The cell containing the polling question spans three rows of the table. The cell containing the label, "Political Party," spans three columns. Finally the title of the table spans both two rows and two columns.

Figure 4-35 ◄
Example of
spanning cells

this cell spans
two columns and
two rows

this cell spans
three columns

this cell spans
three rows

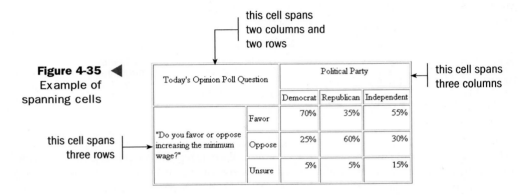

Today's Opinion Poll Question		Political Party		
		Democrat	Republican	Independent
"Do you favor or oppose increasing the minimum wage?"	Favor	70%	35%	55%
	Oppose	25%	60%	30%
	Unsure	5%	5%	15%

The spanning cell in your table will cover the name of the Gargoyle Judge in the last two rows of the table as shown in Figure 4-36.

Figure 4-36 ◄
Table structure
you want
to create

spanning cell

Name	Item #			Price
Bacchus	48059			$95
Praying Gargoyle	48159			$225
Spitting Gargoyle	48184			$200
Gargoyle Judge	48222			$275
Order your gargoyle today!				

Creating a spanning cell with the Netscape Editor can be a confusing process. It involves two steps. The first step is to choose the spanning cell and indicate how many rows and columns that cell will cover. The second step involves "cleaning up" the table so that it matches your intended table structure. Since this final step can involve deleting cells from the table you usually create spanning cells before entering table text.

To see how this works, consider the table structure shown in Figure 4-37 where the cell in the top row of the finished table on the right spans three columns.

Figure 4-37 ◄
Spanning cell

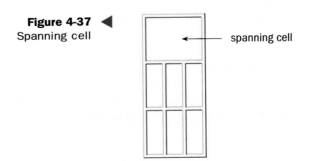

spanning cell

One way of creating this table is to start with the 3x3 table shown in Figure 4-38. To make it easier to understand the process of creating a spanning cell, the cells in the table have been labeled with the numbers 1 through 9. If you want to make this table match the one shown in Figure 4-37, cells 1, 2, and 3 will have to be replaced with a single cell. The first step is to make cell 1 a spanning cell that will span three columns.

Figure 4-38 ◀
Creating a
spanning cell

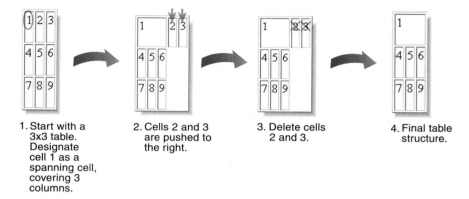

1. Start with a 3x3 table. Designate cell 1 as a spanning cell, covering 3 columns.

2. Cells 2 and 3 are pushed to the right.

3. Delete cells 2 and 3.

4. Final table structure.

After you have designated cell 1 as a spanning cell covering three columns, the Netscape Editor pushes cells 2 and 3 to the right. In order to arrive at the table structure in Figure 4-37, you must remove cells 2 and 3 from the table. Once those cells are deleted the table structure matches the one shown in Figure 4-37.

Designating cell 1 as the spanning cell is important. Because Netscape Editor pushes the old cells to the right, you should designate the cell in the left-most column as the spanning cell. To create a cell that spans several rows, you should designate the top-most cell of that range of rows as the spanning cell.

Creating a cell that spans several rows is a similar process. Figure 4-39 shows the steps involved in creating a cell to span three rows. In this case you designate cell 1 as the spanning cell, which pushes the second two rows of the table to the right. To create the final table structure you delete the two cells in the final column of the last two rows of the table.

Figure 4-39 ◀
Creating a
spanning cell
that spans
rows

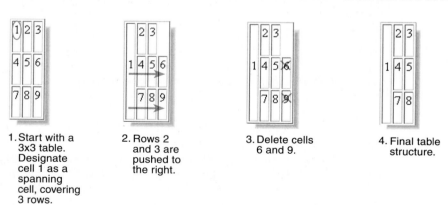

1. Start with a 3x3 table. Designate cell 1 as a spanning cell, covering 3 rows.

2. Rows 2 and 3 are pushed to the right.

3. Delete cells 6 and 9.

4. Final table structure.

You are ready to create a spanning cell in your products table. Because your spanning cell will span two rows in the first column, you choose the upper of those two cells.

To insert a spanning cell:

1. Click the cell in the first column and in the second row from the bottom.

2. Click the **Object Properties** button 🔲.

3. Type **2** in the Cell spans rows box. Figure 4-40 displays the completed dialog box.

Figure 4-40 ◀
Designating
cells to span

cell will span number
of rows entered
here—change this
value to 2

cell will span number
of columns entered
here—leave this
value as 1

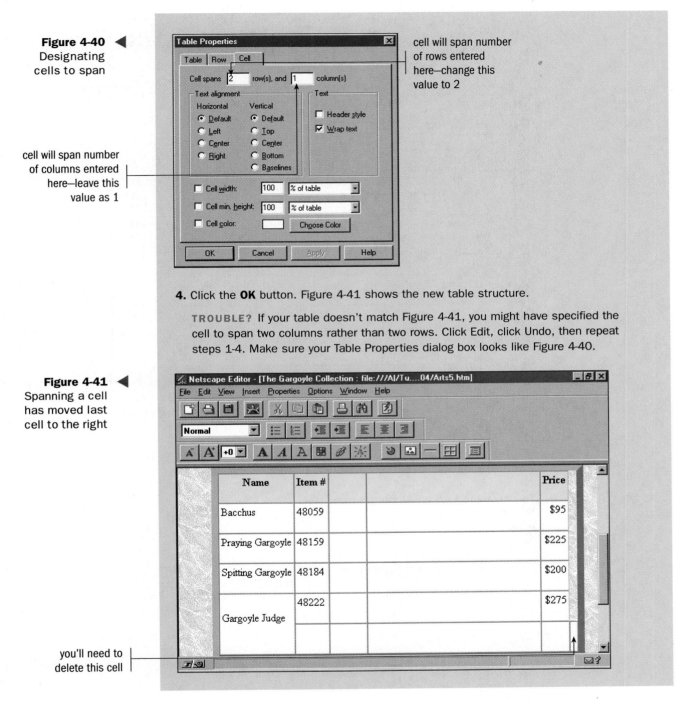

4. Click the **OK** button. Figure 4-41 shows the new table structure.

   TROUBLE? If your table doesn't match Figure 4-41, you might have specified the cell to span two columns rather than two rows. Click Edit, click Undo, then repeat steps 1-4. Make sure your Table Properties dialog box looks like Figure 4-40.

Figure 4-41 ◀
Spanning a cell
has moved last
cell to the right

you'll need to
delete this cell

By creating the spanning cell, the last row of the table has been shifted to the right. To restore your table to the proper structure, you delete the last cell in the bottom row.

To delete the last cell:

1. Click the right-most cell in the bottom row.

2. Click **Edit**, point to **Delete Table**, then click **Cell**. Figure 4-42 shows the final structure of your table.

3. In the bottom row, set the width for the cell in the third column to 50 pixels and the cell in the forth column to 300 pixels using techniques shown earlier in this session.

TROUBLE? If your table does not match the structure shown in Figure 4-42, click Edit then click Undo to restore the previous table structure. Review the steps and try again.

Figure 4-42 ◀
Completed
table structure

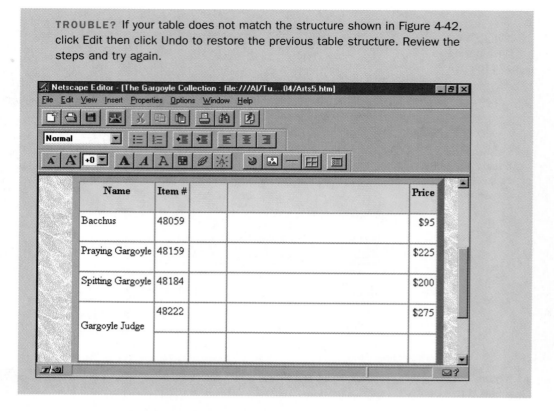

Creating Wrapped Text

With the table structure now in its final form you can enter the table text—the table headers for the two new columns you just created.

To enter the two new column headers:

1. Click the cell in the first row and third column.

2. Type **Image**.

3. Click the **Object Properties** button 🔲, then click the **Cell** tab.

4. Click the **Header style** check box, then click the **OK** button.

5. Click the cell in the first row and fourth column.

6. Type **Description**.

7. Click the **Object Properties** button 🔲, then click the **Cell** tab.

8. Click the **Header style** check box, then click the **OK** button.

The next step is to add information about the new gargoyle item into the table.

To add information about the new gargoyle:

1. Click the cell in the bottom row of the Item # column.

2. Type **48223**.

3. Click the cell in the bottom row of the Price column.

4. Type **$275**. The price value is left-aligned so you will have to align the text with the right side of the table cell.

5. Click the **Object Properties** button 🖾, then click the **Right** option button under Horizontal Alignment.

6. Click the **OK** button. Figure 4-43 displays your table with the newly entered text.

Figure 4-43 ◄
Table with
new entries

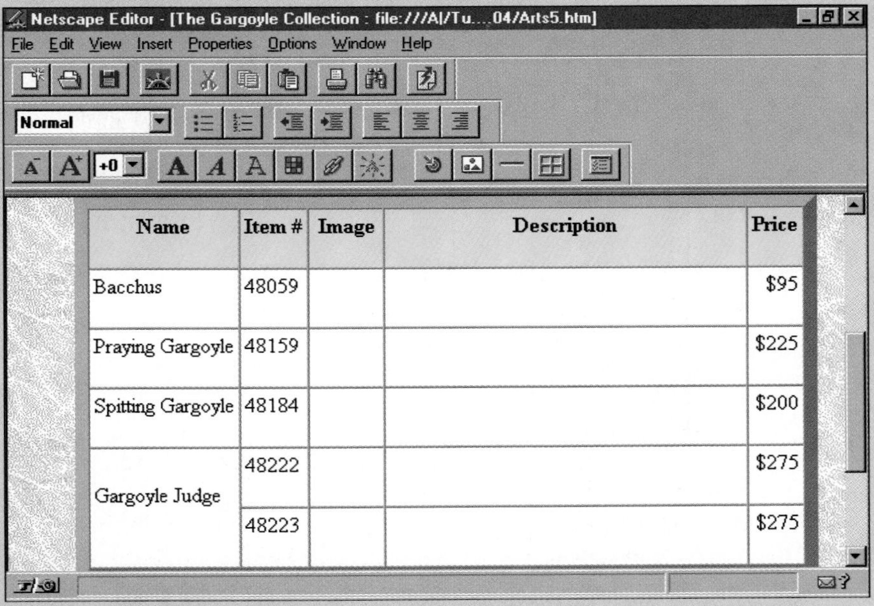

Netscape Editor - [The Gargoyle Collection : file:///A|/Tu....04/Arts5.htm]

File Edit View Insert Properties Options Window Help

Normal

Name	Item #	Image	Description	Price
Bacchus	48059			$95
Praying Gargoyle	48159			$225
Spitting Gargoyle	48184			$200
Gargoyle Judge	48222			$275
	48223			$275

The final column of information you need to enter is the Description column. Until now, the cell width has expanded automatically to accommodate the text you've entered. However, you fixed the Description column at 300 pixels and the width of the overall table at 550 pixels. When you fix the width of a column or table, the column will continue to expand until it surpasses the limits you set for the column or the table. Once it reaches one of those limits, the text will automatically be wrapped to the next line. Since the text that Nicole wants you to place in the Description column is extensive, the editor will have to wrap the text in order to fit it into the confines you set for the table.

To enter the text in the Description column:

1. Click the cell in the Description column for the Bacchus item.

2. Type:

The God of Wine and Joy makes a beautiful ornament on any wall. Interior Plaster. 9"Wx10"Dx12"H

The text automatically wraps to a new line as you type. Figure 4-44 shows the centers of the cell.

Figure 4-44 ◄
Entry in
Description
column

new entry ——————

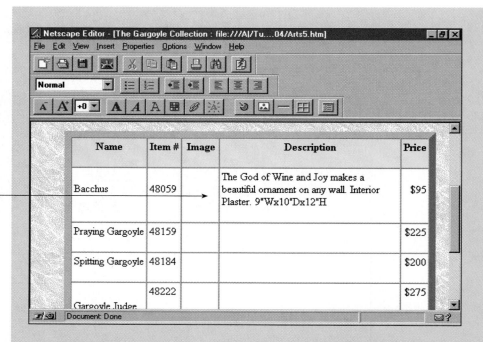

3. Continue to enter descriptive text for the remaining cells in the Description column. Type:

The Praying Gargoyle from the Washington University Cathedral will make a splendid addition to your garden. Gothic Stone. 20"Wx15"Dx24"H

4. Click the next cell down, then type:

One of the most popular of the Notre Dame gargoyles, the Spitting Gargoyle adds its own distinct touch to your garden or lawn. Gothic Stone. 16"Wx20"Dx24"H

5. Click the next cell down, then type:

From the Washington University Cathedral, the Gargoyle Judge remains our most popular item. Interior Plaster. 20"Wx16"Dx20"H

6. Click the last cell then type:

The Gargoyle Judge designed for outdoor use in your garden or lawn. Gothic Stone. 20"Wx16"Dx20"H

7. Compare your table to the version shown in Figure 4-45.

TROUBLE? Some versions of the Netscape Editor have a bug where the text of a table will suddenly appear in bold type. If this happens to you, save the document, click View, then click Reload.

Figure 4-45 ◀
Table with
completed
Description
entries

The Gargoyle Collection

Throughout Europe, countless gargoyles peer down from the towers and parapets of medieval cathedrals. In honor of these fascinating creations, Middle Age Arts presents an exclusive line of gargoyle replicas. Choose representations from the most famous cathedrals in the world, including the popular gargoyles of Notre Dame. Select from the following list of our most popular gargoyles.

Name	Item #	Image	Description	Price
Bacchus	48059		The God of Wine and Joy makes a beautiful ornament on any wall. Interior Plaster. 9"Wx10"Dx12"H	$95
Praying Gargoyle	48159		The Praying Gargoyle from the Washington University Cathedral will make a splendid addition to your garden. Gothic Stone. 20"Wx15"Dx24"H	$225
Spitting Gargoyle	48184		One of the most popular of the Notre Dame gargoyles, the Spitting Gargoyle adds its own distinct touch to your garden or lawn. Gothic Stone. 16"Wx20"Dx24"H	$200
Gargoyle Judge	48222		From the University Cathedral, the Gargoyle Judge remains our most popular item. Interior Plaster. 20"Wx16"Dx20"H	$275
	48223		The Gargoyle Judge designed for outdoor use in your garden or lawn. Gothic Stone. 20"Wx16"Dx20"H	$275

Order your gargoyle today!

Inserting Images into Tables

You can put any Web page element into a table cell, including ordered and unordered lists as well as inline images. Nicole has suggested that you include product photos in the table. These photos have already been scanned for you and saved as GIF images. You can start inserting these images with the Bacchus inline image.

To insert the Bacchus image:

1. Click the cell in the Image column for the Bacchus item.

2. Click the **Insert Image** button ▣.

3. Click the **Browse** button next to the Image File name box.

4. Select the **Bacchus** image file located in the Tutorial.04 folder on your Student Disk, then click the **Open** button.

5. Click the **OK** button. Figure 4-46 shows the Bacchus image as it is inserted into the products table.

Figure 4-46 ◄
Inserting an image into a table

inserted image

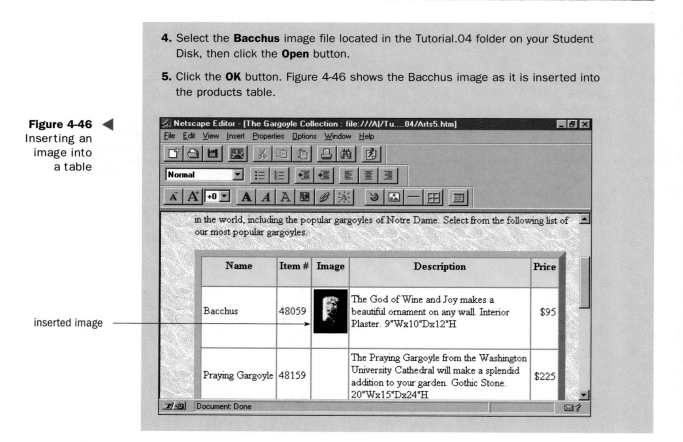

Add the rest of the graphics in the Images column.

To complete the Images column:

1. Insert the image file **Praying** in the row for the Praying Gargoyle.

2. Insert the image file **Spitting** in the row for the Spitting Gargoyle.

3. Insert the image file **Judge** in the row for the first Gargoyle Judge.

4. Insert the image file **Judge2** in the row for the second Gargoyle Judge. Figure 4-47 shows the completed Images column.

Figure 4-47 ◀
Table with
all images
inserted

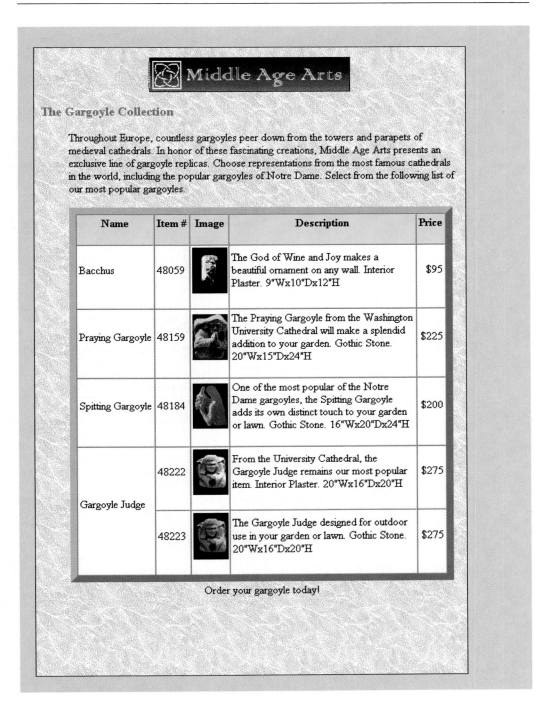

You've completed your work on the Arts5 page. To see the final version of the page, save your page and view it in the Netscape browser.

To view the page in the browser:

1. Click the **Save** button 🖫.

2. Click the **View in Browser** button 🖳. Figure 4-48 shows the completed page as it appears in the browser.

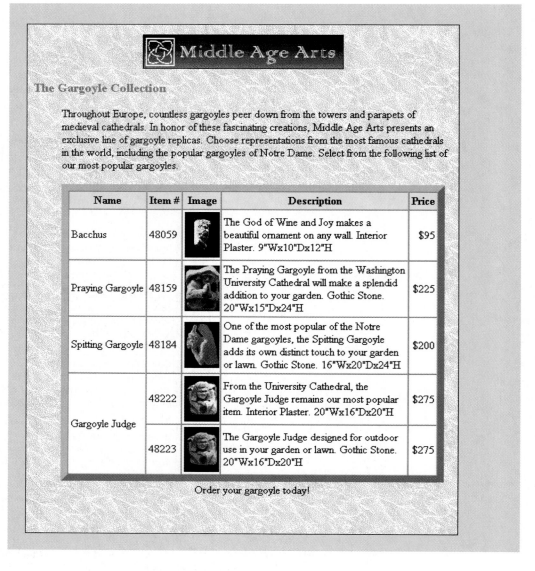

You show the completed page to Nicole. She's pleased with the appearance of the page. She wants to take some more time to review it and will get back to you with her changes. For now you can take a break and exit Netscape.

To exit Netscape:

1. Click **File**, then click **Exit** in the Netscape browser window.

2. When Netscape prompts you to close all windows, click the **Yes** button.

Quick Check

1 Describe how to remove a column from a graphical table.

2 Describe how to insert a column into a graphical table.

3 What is a spanning cell?

4 What are the two steps involved in creating a spanning cell?

5 Under what conditions does the Netscape Editor wrap text within a cell?

6 Describe how to insert an inline image into a graphical table.

Tutorial Assignments

Nicole likes the work you did on the table for the Gargoyle Collection. She would like you to continue working on another table. This time the table will showcase some of the products in the Vatican Collection, a collection of prints and tapestries based on works of art from the Vatican. She has two tables in mind: a text table based on the table shown in Figure 4-49, and a graphical table based on Figure 4-50.

Figure 4-49 ◀

Name	Item #	Type	Price
Christ	92001	Wood Etching	$125
Baptism of Christ	92059	Brass Etching	$100
Keys given to Peter	92180	Tapestry	$165

Figure 4-50 ◀

The Vatican Collection				
Name	Item #	Image	Description	Price
Christ	92001		A wood carving of Christ with crucifix by the noted artist, Francisco Rullini. 12"Wx18"H.	$125
Baptism of Christ	92059		Brass Etching of the baptism of Christ, based on the Vatican tapestry by Perugino and Pinturricchio from the Sistine Chapel. 12"Wx16"H.	$100
Keys given to Peter	92180		Recreation of the Perugino tapestry, "Jesus handing Peter the keys to Heaven," from the Sistine Chapel. 12"Wx15"H.	$165

To complete this tutorial assignment:

1. Open the file, "Vatican," located in the TAssign folder on the Tutorial.04 folder on your Student Disk.
2. Open the Document Properties dialog box and enter your name in the Author box located on the General dialog sheet.
3. Save the file as "Vatican2" in the TAssign folder of the Tutorial.04 folder on your Student Disk.
4. Beneath the description of the table, create a text table using the Formatted Paragraph style.
5. Type the table information displayed in Figure 4-49. Allow for twenty spaces between the Name column and the Item # column, five spaces between the Item # and Type column, and fifteen spaces between the Type and Price column. Use line breaks to insert new rows in the table. To use a line of equal signs (=) to create a horizontal line beneath the table headers.

6. Save your changes to the Vatican2 file.

7. View the new page in the Netscape browser and print out a copy of the page.

8. Open the file, "Vatican3," located in the TAssign folder on the Tutorial.04 folder on your Student Disk.

9. Open the Document Properties dialog box and enter your name in the Author box located on the General dialog sheet.

10. Save the file as "Vatican4" in the TAssign folder on the Tutorial.04 folder on your Student Disk.

11. Insert a 5x5 graphical table beneath the introductory paragraph.

12. Change the properties of the cell in the first row and column of the table, so that it spans 1 row and 5 columns.

13. Delete the four cells pushed to the right edge of the table in the first row.

14. Enter the main table heading, "Vatican Collection," in the first row of the table.

15. Enter each of the five column headings from Figure 4-50 in the second row of the table.

16. Format each cell in the first two rows of the table using the Header Style.

17. Choose each cell in the fourth column of the table (the Description column) and define each length to be 150 pixels. Define the width of the entire table to be 550 pixels.

18. Define the background color for the entire table to be white.

19. Set the Cell Padding to 3 pixels, the Cell Spacing to 2 pixels, and the Border line width to 5 pixels.

20. Define the color for the first two rows of the table to be yellow.

21. Enter the text for the Name, Item #, Description, and Price column, shown in Figure 4-50.

22. Insert the graphic file, "Christ.gif," in the first row of the Image column of the table.

23. Insert the graphic file, "Baptism.gif," in the second row of the Image column.

24. Insert the graphic file, "Keys.gif," in the third row of the Image column.

25. Change the vertical alignment of the text in each row of the table to the top of the cell.

26. Save your changes, then view the page in the Netscape browser.

27. Print a copy of the page to give to your instructor.

Case Problems

1. Creating a Calendar of Activities at Avalon Books You've been asked to create a Web page that displays a calendar of children's activities for the month of May 1998, at Avalon Books. You can create such a calendar using tables. An empty May 1998, calendar is shown in Figure 4-51.

Figure 4-51 ◀

Sunday	Monday	Tuesday	Wednesday	Thursday	Friday	Saturday
				1)	2)	3)
4)	5)	6)	7)	8)	9)	10)
11)	12)	13)	14)	15)	16)	17)
18)	19)	20)	21)	22)	23)	24)
25)	26)	27)	28)	29)	30)	31)

Using the May 1998, calendar as the basis for your table, place the following activities in the appropriate table cells:

- Every Monday: Noon storytime with Susan Sheridan
- Every Friday: Noon storytime with Doug Evans
- May 14 and May 28: Young authors workshop 1 to 4 P.M.
- May 3: Ms. Frizzle of the Magic School Bus pays a visit to teach about science 2 to 3 P.M.
- May 8: Origami with Susan Davis 2 to 3 P.M.
- May 11: Spenser Brown's Clown Show 1 to 2 P.M.
- May 15: Water Color with Susan Davis 2 to 3 P.M.
- May 17: Ecology workshop with Nancy Freis 9 to 11 A.M.
- May 20: Making a model of the solar system 2 to 3 P.M.

To complete this case problem:
1. Open the file, "May.htm", from the Cases folder on the Tutorial.04 folder on your Student Disk.
2. Open the Document Properties dialog box and enter your name in the Author box in the General dialog sheet.
3. Save the file as "May2" in the Cases folder on your Student Disk.
4. Add a 7x7 table after the introductory paragraph.
5. Format each cell in the table to be 80 pixels wide and define the table color to be gray (located in the sixth row and sixth column of the color table).
6. Format the cell in the first row and first column of the table to span over 1 row and seven columns. Delete the extra six columns you create by doing this.
7. Type the title, "Children's Programs at Avalon Books", in the first row of the table.
8. Change the cell width of the cell to 500 pixels.
9. Type the days of the week, starting with Sunday in the second row of the table.
10. Highlight the cells in the table below the header rows and reduce the font size by 2 points.
11. Enter the days of the month starting in the third row of the table as shown in Figure 4-51. Note that May 1st is a Thursday and that May 31st is a Saturday.
12. Enter the activity information listed previously in the appropriate cells of the table. Note that some of the activities are repeated several times throughout the course of the month.
13. Change the vertical text alignment in each row of the table to be aligned with the top of the cell.
14. Format each cell in the first two rows of the table in the Header style.
15. Insert a caption above the table reading, "May 1998."
16. Save your page and view it in the browser.
17. Create a printout of the page and hand it in to your instructor.

2. Inserting a Bulleted List into a Table You can place any page element in a table cell, including bulleted lists. At Wizard Works, the computer superstore that you work for, you have the need to do just that. Your supervisor wants you to create a Web page of their computer products. As part of the table on that page, he wants to place a bulleted list of the features of each computer. The three products in the table are:

Family PC ($2100)

- 100 MHz Pentium processor
- 8 MB RAM
- 1.6 GB EIDE hard drive
- 8x CD-ROM drive
- 15" Super VGA monitor

SOHO PC ($2800)

- 160 MHz Pentium processor
- 16 MB RAM
- 2.1 GB EIDE hard drive
- 8x CD-ROM drive
- 28.8 bps modem
- 17" Super VGA monitor

PC Professional ($3200)

- 200 MHz Pentium Pro processor
- 32 MB RAM
- 2.8 GB SCSI hard drve
- 8x CD-ROM drive
- 28.8 bps modem
- 21" Super VGA monitor

Create a table of the product information placing the product name in the first column, the bulleted list of product features in the second column, and the price in the third column. To complete this case problem:

1. Open the file, "WW.htm," from the Cases folder on the Tutorial.04 folder on your Student Disk.
2. Open the Document Properties dialog box and enter your name in the Author box in the General dialog sheet.
3. Save the file as "WW2" in the Cases folder on your Student Disk.
4. Add a table with 5 rows and 3 columns after the introductory paragraph.
5. Select the cell in the first row and first column of the table and change it to a spanning cell, spanning 1 row and 3 columns. Remove the excess cells in the first row.
6. Type "Wizard Works Computers" in the first row of the table.
7. Enter the names "Model," "Description," and "Price" in the three cells in the second row of the table.
8. Format each cell in the first two rows of the table with the Header style.
9. Enter the model names in the first column of the table.
10. Enter the price values in the third column of the table.
11. Select the Description cell for the Family PC and click the Bullet list button .
12. Type the bulleted list of information about the Family PC.
13. Select the Description cells for the remaining products and enter the bulleted list of features.
14. Save the changes to the WW2 page.
15. View the page in the Netscape browser.
16. Print a copy of the page and hand in the printout to your instructor.

3. Creating a Television Schedule at WMTZ You're in charge of creating Web pages for the television station, WMTZ, in Atlanta. One of these Web pages contains the weekly television listing for each night of the week from 7:00 P.M. to 10:00 P.M. To create this schedule you have to use a graphical table, where each column of the table represents one half hour of programming. Since some programs cover an hour or two, you will have to include spanning cells in the table to cover those time periods. Figure 4-52 shows the schedule for the week of 6/2/98 to 6/8/98.

Figure 4-52 ◀

	7:00	7:30	8:00	8:30	9:00	9:30
Mon.	The Nanny	Dave's World	The Browns	Cybill	Emergency Center	
Tue.	Babylon 5		911 Stories	John Davidson	Mission Impossible	
Wed.	Special: The Budget Crisis		Perfume		48 Hours	
Thu.	Mel's Diner	Alien World	Movie: Wayne's World III			
Fri.	Movie Special: Schindler's List					
Sat.	Dr. Quinn, Medicine Woman		Murder for Hire		New York Streets	
Sun.	Those Dogs!	Wacky People	Movie: Never Say Never Again			

To create this television schedule:

1. Open the file, "WMTZ.htm," from the Cases folder on the Tutorial.04 folder on your Student Disk.
2. Open the Document Properties dialog box and enter your name in the Author box in the General dialog sheet.
3. Save the file as "WMTZ2" in the Cases folder on your Student Disk.
4. Add a table with 8 rows and 7 columns after the horizontal line.
5. Set the border width of the table to 5 pixels, the cell spacing to 3 pixels, and the cell padding to 5 pixels.
6. In the first row of the table, starting with the second column, enter the times from 7:00 to 9:30 in 30 minute increments.
7. In the first column of the table, starting with the second row, enter the three letter abbreviation for each day of the week, starting with Mon.
8. Using the table shown in Figure 4-52 as a guide, insert spanning cells in the appropriate places in the table.
9. Fill in the programming information into the appropriate cells of the table, based on the program names shown in Figure 4-52.
10. Format the cells in the first row and first column of the table with the Header style.
11. Define the color for the first row and first column of the table as yellow.
12. Define the color for all the cells in the first column of the table as yellow.
13. Save your changes to the WMTZ2 file.
14. View the file in the Netscape browser and create a printout of your page.
15. Hand the page in to your instructor.

4. Astonomy Page at Kolbe Middle School You are a science teacher at Kolbe Middle School. As part of a class project on the Solar System, you are creating a Web page with astronomical data about each of the nine planets. Figure 4-53 shows a table of the data you want to include in the page.

Figure 4-53 ◀

Planet	Distance (AU)	Period (yrs)	Mass (Earth=1)	Radius (Earth=1)
Mercury	0.39	0.24	0.06	0.38
Venus	0.72	0.62	0.82	0.95
Earth	1.00	1.00	1.00	1.00
Mars	1.52	1.88	0.11	0.53
Jupiter	5.20	11.86	317.80	11.2
Saturn	9.54	29.46	95.1	9.42
Uranus	19.18	84.01	14.5	4.10
Neptune	30.06	164.79	17.2	3.88
Pluto	29.44	247.7	0.004	0.188

Create two Web pages that showcase this table. The first page should be designed for text-only browsers and contain a text table. The second should use graphical elements and contain a graphical table. Use any design elements or special features that you think will enhance the appearance of the graphical page. You should include images of each of the nine planets in the graphical table. Graphic image files of the planets can be found in the Cases folder on the Tutorial.04 folder on your Student Disk. Your completed Web pages should be saved under the name "Planets" for the text table page and "Planets2" for the graphical table page. Save both of them to the Cases folder on your Student Disk. Be sure to include information about the pages in their Document Properties dialog box.

Answers to Quick Check Questions

SESSION 1.1

1   A network in which the computers are located in a central location such as an office building or computer lab.

2   A system of millions of computer networks linked together in a "network of networks."

3   Unlike CompuServe or America Online, the Internet is a decentralized structure, so finding information can be difficult. The World Wide Web makes it easier to locate information and work with the variety of computers and platforms available on the Internet.

4   A Web server stores the World Wide Web document. A Web browser displays the contents of the document on the user's computer.

5   Hypertext links are text items that when selected by a mouse or other pointing device jump the user to a different place in the document, to a new document, or to a new computer.

6   Either the first page you see when you start your Web browser or the page that represents you or your company's interests.

SESSION 1.2

1   The Netscape Page Wizard is just a page on the World Wide Web.

2   Frames are sections of a document window that can contain their own scroll bars and hypertext links.

3   It creates a Web page based on your specifications from the Page Wizard.

4   Four

5   A page title, introductory text, closing paragraph, hypertext link list, e-mail link

SESSION 1.3

1   No

2   Highlight text to be replaced and type the new text over the selected old text.

3   Use the browser to display the page, then click the Edit button the Netscape toolbar and save the page and any attached files to your hard drive or floppy disk.

4   Click Help and then click Handbook from the Netscape menu.

SESSION 2.1

1   Templates are predesigned Web pages you can access by clicking File, New Document, then From Template.

2   So that people using different Web search tools will have greater chance of finding your page.

3   The Paragraph Format toolbar formats entire paragraphs. The File/Edit toolbar is for file management tasks. The Character Format toolbar formats text and other objects.

4   A label used in HTML to indicate the appearance of each element on a Web page.

5   A paragraph tag is a markup tag applied to an entire paragraph. A character tag is a markup tag applied to a word, phrase, or character.

6   The Netscape Editor generally formats the page, but the ultimate appearance of the page is determined by the Web browser. A word processor specifically formats the page's appearance.

7   If you could create your own tags, other Web browsers wouldn't be able to read your page.

SESSION 2.2

1   With a # symbol in the Editor and with the appropriate number in the browser.

2   Select the list items and right-click your selection. Choose Paragraph/List properties from the popup menu. Click a new bullet from the Bullet Style list box.

3   It is 3 points larger than normal text.

4   Select the text you want to change, right-click the selection, and choose Character Properties from the popup menu. In the Character Properties dialog box make all the formatting changes you need to make.

5   Select the text you want to change, and click the Font Color button on the Character Format toolbar. Choose the appropriate color from the color list.

SESSION 2.3

1 An inline graphic appears on the page, while an external graphic is displayed by an application called a viewer, which appears separate from the page.

2 JPG and GIF.

3 An noninterlaced graphic appears one line at a time, starting from the top of the image and working down. In an interlaced graphic, the image appears stepwise with the image gradually getting into focus.

4 Right-click the line and choose Horizontal Line properties. Enter 25 in the Width box and choose % of Window as the width option.

5 Because you can't see the effect of text wrapping in the Editor—only in the browser.

6 That the graphic image is not so large that it makes the page take longer to display and that it is not too distracting from the main text on the page.

SESSION 3.1

1 A target is a reference point on a page that identifies a specific location. A link is spot on the page that jumps the user to the target.

2 Highlight the text or element that you want to act as a target and click the Insert Target button on the Character Format toolbar. Enter a name for the target.

3 Case sensitive.

4 Highlight the text, click the Make Link button on the Character Format toolbar, and specify the location to jump to.

5 Click the Make Link button on the Character Format toolbar, enter the hypertext in the text box, and specify the location to jump to.

SESSION 3.2

1 Storyboarding is the technique of creating a graphical representation of the pages and links in a Web presentation. Storyboarding is important is creating a coherent and user-friendly structure.

2 A linear structure is one in which Web pages are linked from one to another in a direct chain. Users can go to the previous page or next page in the chain, but not to a page in a different section of the chain.

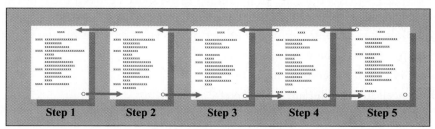

You could use a linear structure in a Web page presentation that included a series of steps that the user must follow, such as in a recipe or instructions to complete a task.

3 A hierarchical structure is one in which Web pages are linked from general to specific topics. Users can move up and down the hierarchy tree.

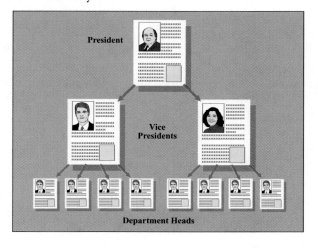

A company might use such a structure to describe the management organization.

4   Click the Make Link button, click the Browse File button, and locate the file that you want to link to.

5   Click the Make Link button, click the Browse File button, and locate the file that you want to link to. Within that file, choose from the target list the specific location in the document that you want to link to.

SESSION 3.3

1   The communications protocol, the Internet host name, the folder containing the document, the filename of the document, any target in the document.

2   http://www.ftd.com/flowers/inventory/info.htm

3   ftp://ftp.umich.edu

4   news:rec.sports.basketball.pro

5   mailto:baker@csw.edu

SESSION 4.1

1   A text table is a table that uses only text characters to display and format the table. A graphical table uses graphical elements. You would use a text table rather than a graphical table if you need to have your page viewed by text-based browsers.

2   A fixed width allots the same space to each character; a proportional font allots space based on the letter width.

3   If the table is viewed under different font sizes, the columns may lose alignment.

4   A nonbreaking space is a space between words that will allow for multiple spaces.

5   A line break is an inserted line that remains with the current paragraph rather than starting a new paragraph.

6   The formatted paragraph style formats text with fixed width fonts and interprets all spaces as nonbreaking spaces.

SESSION 4.2

1   Cells that contain headings for rows or columns. You create a table head by selecting a cell and clicking the Properties button. You then click the Header Style check box or the cell sheet.

2   Cell spacing is the space between the cells. Cell padding is the space between the cell text and the cell boundary. The table border is the width of the outside boundary of the table.

3   You can specify table size in absolute terms in number of pixels, or as a percentage of the display area.

4   Set the table width to 100% of the window in size.

5   Set the width of every cell in the column to 250 pixels.

6   Set the width of one cell in the column to 250 pixels.

SESSION 4.3

1   Select a cell from the column, and click Edit, Delete Table, and Column.

2   Select a cell to the left of the place where you want to insert the new column and click Insert, Table, and Column.

3   A cell that spans multiple rows and/or columns.

4   Indicate the number of rows and/or columns that the cell will span and then remove extra rows or columns created by inserting the spanning cell.

5   When the width of the column has been fixed and it can not increase any further to encompass the additional text.

6   Click the cell in which the image should be placed and then click the Insert Image button, specify the location of the graphic file, and click the OK button.

Index

Netscape Navigator Gold Task Reference

TASK	PAGE #	RECOMMENDED METHOD	NOTES
Background, set properties	NG 75	Click Properties, Document, click the Appearance tab, choose a background image from a graphics file or choose a color.	See "Using a Graphic Image as a Page Background"
Bullet Style, change	NG 60	Select the bulleted list, right-click the selection and click Paragraph/List properties. Select a bullet style from the Bullet style list.	
Cell color, set		Click the cell, click the Object Properties button ⊞, click the Cell tab, click the Choose Color button, choose a color from the color list.	
Cell padding, set size	NG 137	Click any cell within the table, click the Object Properties button ⊞, click the Table tab, enter the cell padding size in the Cell padding text box.	
Cell spacing, set size	NG 137	Click any cell within the table, click the Object Properties button ⊞, click the Table tab, enter the cell spacing size in the Cell spacing text box.	
Character tags, apply	NG 62	Select the text, click a button from the Character Format toolbar.	See "Applying Character Tags"
Character tags, apply multiple	NG 65	Select the text, right-click the selection, click Character Properties.	
Document Properties, set	NG 50	Click Properties, Document.	
Font color, change	NG 64	Select the text, click the Font Color button ⊞, choose a color.	
Font size, increase or decrease	NG 63	Select the text, click the Increase font size button A' to increase the font size, click the Decrease font size button A to decrease the font size.	
Font, apply fixed width	NG 121	Select the text, click the Fixed Width button A.	
Font, bold	NG 62	Select the text, click the Bold button A.	
Font, italicize	NG 62	Select the text, click the Italic button A.	
Graphical table, create	NG 127	Click the Insert Table button ⊞.	See "Creating a Graphical Table"
Help, start	NG 40	Click Help, Handbook.	
Horizontal Line, insert	NG 67	Click the Insert Horiz. Line button —.	See "Inserting a Horizontal Line"
Horizontal Line, set properties	NG 69	Right-click the horizontal line, click Horizontal Line Properties.	
Hypertext link, activate	NG 12	Move pointer over the link until the pointer shape changes to a 👆 and click.	
Hypertext link, create between documents	NG 99	Select the text to be made into hypertext, click the Make Link button 🔗, click the Browse File button, select the file you want to link to, click any target within that document.	See "Creating a Hypertext Link to Another Document"
Hypertext link, create in same document	NG 88	Select the text to be made into hypertext, click the Make Link button 🔗 and choose a target from the current document.	See "Creating a Hypertext Link to a Target in the Same Document"
Hypertext link, create to FTP server	NG 109	Select the text to be linked, click the Make Link button 🔗, enter the URL of the FTP server.	The form of the URL is ftp://ftp_servername
Hypertext link, create to Gopher server	NG 110	Select the text to be linked, click the Make Link button 🔗, enter the URL of the Gopher server.	The form of the URL is gopher://gophername
Hypertext link, create to newsgroup	NG 110	Select the text to be linked, click the Make Link button 🔗, enter the URL of the USENET newsgroup.	The form of the URL is news:newsgroup

Netscape Navigator Gold 3 Task Reference

TASK	PAGE #	RECOMMENDED METHOD	NOTES
Hypertext link, create to e-mail address	NG 111	Select the text to be linked, click the Make Link button 🔗, enter the URL of the e-mail address.	The form of the URL is mailto: *mail_address*
Hypertext link, create to Internet document	NG 105	Select the text to be made into hypertext, click the Make Link button 🔗, enter the URL of the document you want to link to.	See "Creating a Hypertext Link to a Document on the Internet"
Hypertext link, create with drag and drop	NG 106	Select a link on another Web page, drag and drop the link onto the page you're working on in the Editor.	
Inline image, insert	NG 72	Click the Insert Image button 🖼 and browse your hard drive to find the image file.	See "Inserting an Inline Image"
Inline image, set properties	NG 74	Click the inline image and click the Object Properties 🖼 button.	
Line breaks, create	NG 122	Hold down the Shift key and press the Enter key.	See "Inserting Nonbreaking Spaces and Line Breaks"
Netscape browser, start	NG 10	Double-click the Netscape icon 🧭 or open the Netscape program folder and then double-click the Netscape icon 🧭.	See "Starting Netscape Navigator Browser"
Netscape Editor, start	NG 35	Start the Netscape browser, click File, New Document, Blank to open the Editor to a blank page, or click the Edit button to edit the current Web page, or click File, Open File in Editor to open the Editor to a file.	See "Starting the Netscape Editor"
Netscape, exit	NG 15	Click the Close button ❌ on the title bar.	Click File, Exit from the menu.
New Document, create	NG 49	Start the Netscape browser, click File, New Document, Blank.	See "Starting the Netscape Editor"
Nonbreaking spaces, create	NG 123	Hold down the Shift key and press the Spacebar key.	See "Inserting Nonbreaking Spaces and Line Breaks"
Ordered list, create	NG 57	Click the Numbered List button 📋, type each entry, press Enter.	See "Creating an Ordered List"
Page elements, remove	NG 39	Select the page element and press the Delete key.	
Page Wizard, add a background pattern	NG 29	Click the Background Pattern link in the Instructions frame, choose a background from the background list in the Choices frame.	
Page Wizard, add a hypertext link	NG 24	Click the Add Some Hot Links to Other Web Pages link in the Instructions frame, delete the default link and text description, enter your new link and description, click the Apply button.	You can only add up to four hypertext links.
Page Wizard, add an e-mail link	NG 27	Click the Add an E-mail Link link in the Instructions frame, delete the default e-mail address, enter a new address, click the Apply button.	
Page Wizard, add page contents	NG 21	Click an option in the Instructions frame, delete the default text in the Choices frame, enter the text you want on your page, click the Apply button.	See "Adding Page Contents using the Page Wizard"
Page Wizard, build a page	NG 32	Click the Build button in the Instructions frame.	See "Building and Saving your Web Page"
Page Wizard, change an element's color	NG 29	Click one of the page elements listed in the Instructions frame, choose a color from the color list in the Choices frame.	
Page Wizard, choose a bullet style	NG 30	Click the Choose a Bullet Style link in the Instructions frame, choose a bullet from the bullet list in the Choices frame.	
Page Wizard, choose a line style	NG 31	Click the Choose a Horizontal Rule Style link in the Instructions frame, choose a line from the line style list in the Choices frame.	

Netscape Navigator Gold 3 Task Reference

TASK	PAGE #	RECOMMENDED METHOD	NOTES
Page Wizard, correct text	NG 23	Click the option in the Instructions frame that you want to change, delete the old text in the Choices frame, enter the new text, click the Apply button.	
Page Wizard, enter a closing paragraph	NG 23	Click the Type a Paragraph of Text to Serve as a Conclusion link in the Instructions frame, delete the default conclusion, enter your new conclusion, click the Apply button.	
Page Wizard, enter a page title	NG 21	Click the Give Your Page a Title link in the Instructions frame, delete the default title, enter your new title, click the Apply button.	
Page Wizard, enter introductory text	NG 22	Click the Type an Introduction link in the Instructions frame, delete the default introduction, enter your new introduction, click the Apply button.	
Page Wizard, remove a hypertext link	NG 26	Click the Delete Hot Links link in the Choices frame, click the check box of the link you want to remove.	See "Removing a Link"
Page Wizard, save a page	NG 33	Build your page, click the Edit button on the Netscape toolbar, click the Save button.	See "Buidling and Saving your Web Page"
Page Wizard, select a preset color combination	NG 28	Click the A Preset Color Combination link in the Instructions frame, choose a color combination from the list presented in the Choices frame.	
Page Wizard, start	NG 18	Click File, New Document, From Wizard.	See "Creating a Web Page with the Page Wizard"
Page, save	NG 56	Click the Save button .	
Row color, set	NG 138	Click any cell within the row, click the Object Properties button and click the Row tab, click the Choose Color button, choose a color from the color list.	
Style, apply	NG 53	Select the paragraph, click the Paragraph style list arrow, select a style.	See "Applying a Style"
Table border, set size	NG 137	Click any cell within the table, click the Object Properties button , click the Table tab, enter the table border size in the Table Border text box.	
Table caption, create	NG 132	Click any cell within the table, click the Object Properties button , click the table dialog sheet tab, click the Include Caption check box, indicate whether the caption will be above or below the table.	
Table cell, delete	NG 145	Click the cell, click Edit, Delete Table, Cell.	
Table cell, insert		Click a cell to the immediate left of the new cell and click Insert, Table, Cell.	
Table cell, span	NG 144	Click the cell, click the Object Properties button , click the Cell tab, enter the number of rows and columns the cell spans.	
Table colors, set	NG 138	Click any cell within the table, click the Object Properties button , click the Table tab, click the Choose Color button, choose a color from the color list.	
Table column, delete	NG 141	Click a cell in the column, click Edit, Delete Table, Column.	
Table column, insert	NG 142	Click a cell to the immediate left of the new column and click Insert, Table, Column.	
Table column, set size	NG 135	Click a cell within the column, click the Object Properties button , click the Cell tab, click the Cell Width check box, enter the size of the cell, indicating whether this is in pixels or as a percentage of the window size. Continue doing this for each cell in the column.	
Table headings, create	NG 131	Click a cell, click the Object Properties button , click the Header Style check box.	

Netscape Navigator Gold 3 Task Reference

TASK	PAGE #	RECOMMENDED METHOD	NOTES
Table row, delete		Click a cell in the row, click Edit, Delete Table, Row.	
Table row, insert	NG 142	Click a cell immediately above the new row and click Insert, Table, Row.	
Table text, insert	NG 129	Type the text in each cell, press the Up or Down arrow to move between cells.	
Table, delete		Click a cell in the table, click Edit, Delete Table, Table.	
Table, set size	NG 134	Click any cell within the table, click the Object Properties button 🔲, click the Table tab, click the Table Width check box, enter the size of the table, indicating whether this is in pixels or as a percentage of the window size.	
Target, create	NG 85	Select the text to act as a target, click the Insert Target button 🖐 and enter the name of the target.	See "Creating Targets"
Template, access	NG 46	Connect to the Internet, open the Netscape browser, click File, New Document, From Template.	See "Accessing a Netscape Template"
Text table, create	NG 124	Click the Fixed Width button 🅰, use nonbreaking spaces to create spaces between the table columns, use line breaks to start new rows in the table.	See "Creating a Text Table"
Text, center align	NG 54	Select the text, click the Center button 🔲.	
Text, edit	NG 38	Select the old text with the mouse, type new text in its place.	
Text, indenting	NG 61	Select the text, click the Increase Indent button 📑.	
Text, insert	NG 38	Click the spot to where the text will be inserted and type.	
Text, left align	NG 55	Select the text, click the Align Left button 📑.	
Text, right align	NG 55	Select the text, click the Align Right button 📑.	
Text, set properties	NG 60	Right-click the text, click Properties, set properties, click the OK button.	
Unordered list, create	NG 59	Click the Numbered List button 📑, type each entry, press Enter.	See "Creating an Unordered List"
Web Page, print	NG 34	Click File, Print.	
Web pages, move forward	NG 14	Click the Forward button 🔘.	
Web pages, open a specific URL	NG 14	Click the Open button 🔘, enter the URL.	See "Opening a Web Page Using its URL"
Web pages, view previous	NG 14	Click the Back button 🔘.	
Web pages, view your home page.	NG 14	Click the Home button 🔘.	